Where Does A Mother Go to Resign?

BARBARA JOHNSON

Where Does A Mother Go to Resign?

 BETHANY HOUSE
PUBLISHERS
Minneapolis, MN 55438

Where Does a Mother Go to Resign?
Copyright © 1979
Barbara Johnson
New edition 1994

Cover by Koechel Peterson Design, Minneapolis, Minnesota

Published by Bethany House Publishers
A Ministry of Bethany Fellowship International
11400 Hampshire Avenue South
Minneapolis, Minnesota 55438
www.bethanyhouse.com

Printed in the United States of America by
Bethany Press International, Minneapolis, Minnesota 55438

Library of Congress Cataloging-in-Publication Data

Johnson, Barbara E.
    Where does a mother go to resign?
    1. Johnson, Barbara E. 2. Mothers—United States—Biography. 3. Housewives—United States—Biography.
4. Homosexuals, Male—United States—Family relationships.
I. Title.
HQ759.J62   301.42'7   79–12686
ISBN 0–7642–2373–9   CIP

Contents

Foreword

Barbara Johnson is a remarkable woman with a remarkable story of triumph over despair, a story of God's grace operating in the middle of devastating tragedy. Barbara Johnson's testimony today is full of the joy of the Lord.

I first knew Barbara as the "lady with the sunshine smile" at our Christian Center's hotline office. Later I learned of how God had, unknowingly to me, spoken to her through my Bible class to help her through the hard time when she first knew that her son was a homosexual. She has been one of the most faithful members of the Bible class. She has shared tapes of the class with others who are hurting.

It is Barbara's ability to see laughter in all situations, while carefully keeping God's will foremost, that has given her the courage and wisdom to endure the darts of the enemy for so long.

Barbara knows about sleepless nights and cloudy days. She knows agony and grief firsthand. But she also knows the love and comfort of the Lord in the midst of the fire, and the ultimate victory over depression that He provides for the believer who trusts in Him. Using God's Word as her guide, Barbara has told her story for the benefit of thousands of Christians needing God's direction in a desperate situation.

Here at Christian Research Institute and at church, we continually refer those with special needs to Barbara and her ministry. God has blessed her work and will continue to bless it because it meets very specific needs.

Read this book if you are hurting, if your family is hurting, or if you want to learn about triumph in tragedy, about the healing of a broken heart. At one time, Barbara wanted to resign from being a mother. Along with the hundreds who have been helped by her, I am glad that she didn't!

Walter Martin
Anaheim, California
December 4, 1978

A Word from the Author

Fifteenth Anniversary Edition of
Where Does a Mother Go to Resign?

Recently when I was the guest on a *Focus on the Family* broadcast, the staff surprised me with a telephone conversation they had arranged with my son Larry as a special treat for part of the program.

Among other things, Larry said, "We're all grateful for God's healing and restoration. . . ." This might not seem like a noteworthy event or a particularly memorable conversation . . . *except* that this was "Larry," the son in *Where Does a Mother Go to Resign?* He was the pivotal reason why Spatula Ministries was launched over 15 years ago.

At that time there were no books, no ministries to help Christian families who discovered that homosexuality had hit their nice, safe, protected families.

Because my husband and I had no understanding of how to deal with this devastating, painful news, we lived through 11 years of bitter estrangement. This was as agonizing for our son as it was for us.

But even through that incredible pain, we set out on a personal journey of restoration. As we began sharing our story through Spatula Ministries, we reached out to parents who needed "scraping off the ceiling"—which is where they land when they discover that homosexuality has hit them. Through this book and subsequent ones I have written, and through referrals from Focus on the Family and other Christian organizations, we have seen restoration occur in thousands of families. Many others have written to say that our story gave them the first glimmer of hope—that someone actually had survived what they were going through.

Even during those 11 years when our son was gone from us, the Lord kept wrapping us in His comfort blanket and injecting joy into our lives. It spilled over to other parents in pain so that they too could learn to laugh again. *Where Does a Mother Go to Resign?* was written over 15 years ago out of terrible anguish and sorrow, but God has turned it to joy. I know that this new edition can accomplish that for you too.

Joyfully!
Barbara Johnson
The Geranium Lady
April 15, 1994

1

Yankee Doodle, Tinker Bell and One Flat-Out Mom

It was a hot Saturday in June, 1975, the day before Father's Day. I was scurrying to get myself on the way to the Los Angeles airport to pick up my sister, Janet, and her husband, Mel, who were en route to Minneapolis from Hawaii, and were stopping to spend 24 hours with us. We planned to celebrate the evening at Disneyland, spend the night in a motel in Anaheim, and then have a Father's Day dinner together on Sunday before they left.

As I was dashing out the door, the phone rang. It was a friend of Larry's asking to borrow a certain book and wanting to pick it up right away. Impatiently, I rifled through Larry's bookcase and then pulled open the large side drawer in his desk where the huge, red book was lying.

Happy to have located it so quickly, I lifted it out, but as I did my eyes caught some magazines and papers lying under the book. In the stack, about six inches high, were pictures of nude men and a packet of letters, evidently from dealers who sold literature on homosexuality. The envelopes had been addressed to Larry at a post office box in a nearby town.

A wave of nausea swept over me. Surely he was using this material for some school project on this subject. Larry, our third son, was twenty and in his third year of college; surely there had to be a reason why he would have all this material stashed away.

Suddenly, I remembered someone was hanging on the telephone, waiting to know if I had located the book. I managed to conclude the conversation and hung up the phone in a daze of emotions.

I returned to Larry's room and fingered lightly through the advertisements for homosexual films, pictures and other materials. Even touching the stuff I felt as if I were contaminating myself. What was this all about? There had to be a reason why Larry would order these books or be reading about homosexuality. I threw myself down on the bed and a terrible roaring sob burst from me. I was alone in the house, and for several terrifying minutes sobs from fear, shock and disbelief shook me.

Flashing in my mind was this wonderful son who was so bubbly and happy—such a joy to have around. Thinking of him entwined with some other male brought heaves of heavy sobbing from deep wounds of agony.

My reeling thoughts were interrupted by the realization that I had to get to the airport, no matter what state my emotions were in. I thought, "If only I can zip up my questions and all the panic until twenty-four hours from now when the relatives are safely on their way out of here, then surely Larry and I can have a talk, and he will have a logical explanation for this."

Perhaps he had a friend whom he was trying to help. That was Larry, always wanting to help someone else. I snatched the literature and letters from the bed and tossed them all in a sack, thinking I'd keep them with me where they'd be safe—safe from what?

My head felt like a pressure cooker about to explode. How could I let him know that I had found the magazines, but still go through with our plans for Disneyland tonight? Tears were still flowing down my cheeks and my hand was shaking as I took a pen and wrote hurriedly.

Larry, I found the magazines and stuff in the drawer. I love you and God loves you, but this is so wrong. Can we just get through tonight and, after the relatives leave tomorrow, talk about it? Please meet us at the flagpole at Disneyland at 8:00 so we can enjoy the big Centennial parade and fireworks with them anyway.

I tried to reread the scribbled note but the sobbing inside made my writing look like that of a trembling senile. In my mind was the pressure of getting to the airport and meeting the plane. "If we can just get through the next 24 hours, then I can die tomorrow," I thought. I felt as if my legs had been amputated, but there was no way to stop the bleeding until tomorrow. But *how* could anyone survive a full day with such pain in her heart and waves of nausea flowing over it?

That drive to the Los Angeles airport was only a blur. I alternated with heaving sobs of stabbing pain to low moans like those of a dying person. This was not really happening—surely I could push back the clock one hour before and remember the fun and excitement we always had at Disneyland.

Why couldn't we have just this one day together to make some good memories for us all, since it was the first time our family had been together since Tim's death two years ago? But this *was* happening. It was not a dream. I drove almost in a stupor with little regard for speed or safety. Certainly if a policeman had stopped me and seen my glazed eyes and tear-streaked face, with my "spacey" look, he would have taken me to the nearest hospital. I wondered, "Do they have places where people go who are frozen solid on the panic button?" The pain in my chest was stabbing. My head was throbbing and my throat felt as if it were stuffed with a shag rug eight feet wide. My mind whirled with thoughts of Larry—so irresistible as a little boy, so clever in his repartee, excelling in everything he did.

Janet and Mel arrived on the plane from Hawaii, complete with a crate of pineapples and leis for me. I managed a sick smile and excused my looks and behavior by saying I had *swallowed* something which was making me sick. *Swallowed* was a good word! I was choking inside, dying, I think, but telling myself that for 24 hours I had to put on the best act of my entire life. Besides, I kept telling myself, there might be an explanation for this and all my panic would be for nothing. I knew this was like grabbing a handful of fog, but at this point I would clutch at anything to excuse Larry.

While we were getting the luggage, Janet pumped me for some additional reason for my swollen eyes and blanched face. I said something light about Larry giving us some hassles about wanting to go on a tour with a singing group for the summer, and we couldn't afford it this year. Her response was: "Certainly nothing could be wrong with Larry. He's so loving, so kind, such a blessing. How could *he* ever cause you to be upset?" Janet was sure he could do no wrong.

Driving from the airport to the motel in Anaheim, I was able to lock up my panic and listen to Janet and Mel as they anticipated the excitement of the evening at Disneyland. They commented on what fun it was going to be to spend the evening and have dinner with us on Sunday. It was as if my mind were on automatic pilot, saying words which must have fit into the conversation, but inside my head there was a steady whirl of "homosexuality, homosexuality, homosexuality."

We settled in at the motel with a couple hours to spare before we drove over to meet the rest of the family at the Disneyland flagpole. My husband, Bill, was driving straight from work, Larry was coming from our home, and our youngest son, Barney, who was 17, had secured a ride with a friend. This happened to be the first night of Disneyland's new Electric Parade, with a special fireworks show and all the ballyhoo which goes with the summer opening of the park. Since this was the big Bicentennial celebration it was a Yankee Doodle time with the Disneyland sign blazing, "Celebrate Yankee Doodle with the New Electric Parade."

Splashing cold water on my face and eyes helped reduce the swelling some, and as I freshened up at the motel I kept telling myself that I had to hold it together, no matter how much I was falling apart inside. My sister, who has a keen insight into my psyche, sensed that I was dissolving like wet paper towels inside. I asked her to please not ask me about anything until the evening was over. We could talk when we were alone. Her husband is a successful minister and has had a terrific work with young people, but he was as unfamiliar with homosexuality as I was at that point. The discussion would have to wait until afterward. It was time to leave for Disneyland.

We drove across the immense parking lot to the Disneyland entrance, and I gave Janet and Mel my "Magic Kingdom" card so they could get in without having to walk so far. Then I proceeded to locate a parking spot. I passed by the signs which indicated emergency parking and parking for the handicapped, thinking that I could easily qualify. If there had been a sign saying, "For people in various stages of panic. . . ."

When Janet and Mel got out of the car, I felt sort of relieved. I could give vent to some of the pressure inside me. This concrete brick which had settled in my chest was beginning to make it hard to breathe. My head felt like a melon from crying so much. I had to park the car a mile or so from the main entrance and as I sat there gathering strength for that long walk to the park, I wondered if possibly some tourist might run over me, or if with a stroke of luck the Disneyland trolley might snag me on the cow-catcher so that I would never have to reach that flagpole and the encounter with Larry.

My prayers turned into one, "O Lord, help me get through tonight somehow!" This one thought was paramount in my tired head. All I looked forward to was the possibility of dying tomorrow. But first we had to get through tonight and until 2 P.M. Sunday when the relatives were leaving. Walking to the entrance, so many thoughts flitted through my mind. How could I erase myself from the world? Tomorrow was Father's Day. Our family was together to enjoy the opening summer night at fabulous Disneyland. Homosexuality—what is it? Why would Larry have that collection of stuff?

My feet dragged along the parking lot as if they had bowling balls chained to them. Perhaps I had been too busy in our tape ministry with grieving parents to notice what was happening to Larry. It must have been something I did, or failed to do. It couldn't have simply "happened" like a spontaneous evil growth.

What about Bill? How would he cope with this new trauma? He would be at the flagpole to meet us, completely oblivious to what I had discovered. How could I explain my wan, grief-stricken appearance to him? Maybe he would believe the story that I had choked on something I wasn't able to swallow—which was so true. Oh, so true!

I was grateful for that long walk from the car to the Disneyland entrance. What did I know about homosexuality? I thought back to a boy I knew in the Christian college I attended who was the only homosexual I ever heard of, and he disappeared from home after his parents learned of his problem. What is this gay business? Who are these people who call themselves gay? I thought of a play I'd seen in high school, called

"Our Hearts Were Young and Gay." When had that word changed to something so vile and repugnant as homosexual? But Larry is a *Christian*. Do Christians struggle with this? How can a Christian be a homosexual? Is it mental illness? Is it sin? Is it demonic? Is it an emotional breakdown? None of these categories fit Larry. He knew the Bible and his life had been a testimony to God's redeeming grace.

Could it be possible that Larry was having a struggle with homosexuality during his teenage years and we were too wrapped up in our ministry to notice? Flashing in my mind was an episode which occurred a few months back, when he wanted one of his friends to spend Easter week with us. I had agreed to the weekend but having him for the whole week posed some inconveniences. Larry had stood in the doorway as I was putting on some make-up and he said, "You've got Dad, and Barney has his girl, but I don't have anyone. Don't you see, Mom?"

Without hesitation, I blurted out, "Why, Larry, you have *everything!* You've been on singing tours to Russia, Japan and all over. You have scholarships for college, and so many friends. You are loved by all of us. You have the world by the tail."

Instead of really hearing what he was saying, I sloughed it off, reassuring him of how popular he was in our eyes. So my thoughts tumbled on. Was he then feeling isolated and struggling with homosexuality? How my answer must have grated if he is in its vise-like grip!

Somewhere I had read that there was a course for parents on "How to Stir Up a Fuss in the Right Way at the Right Time about the Right Things." I wondered if they had a corresponding course in "How to Avoid a Fuss in the Right Way at the Right Time about the Wrong Things!"

I was almost to the turnstile at the front gate of the park, and all I had hoped for hadn't happened. It was crowded. The Rapture didn't occur on my pilgrimage over. No trolley or bus had run over me. No wayward tourist had plowed into me in all the crowded lanes. The flagpole encounter was inevitable.

It was as if I were in a long, dark tunnel with no light at the end. A tall flagpole maybe, but no light. In the distance, past all the throngs of people shoving to get through the turnstile, I saw that red, white and blue flag waving high in the Disneyland circle.

How many times I had gone through the Disneyland entrance and heard the song, "When You Wish Upon a Star, Makes No Difference Who You Are...." When I heard it that night I wondered if being homosexual would matter. Can they wish on stars too? How many homosexuals had come through there? Maybe half the world was homosexual and I didn't know it. If my own son could be one and I didn't know it, who knows who else could be? Maybe Mickey Mouse and Donald Duck? Tinker Bell? Suddenly, realizing that normal thoughts were absent from my mind, I had to pray for God to help me bring my thoughts into captivity. My early training had included much Scripture memorization, and now the Lord was reminding me of that portion in 2 Corinthians 10:5 about "bringing into captivity every thought to the obedience of Christ." I had to stop this all-consuming thought of homosexuality. After all, finding some magazines and pictures didn't *prove* anything, did it? There had to be some other reason why Larry had that material in his desk drawer. My thought had gone full circle back to my one shred of hope.

Just getting through the crowd took a bit of doing. Excited people were lining up for the big parade. It seemed that everyone had on Mickey Mouse hats with the big ears, or paper bands around their head, a blue feather stuck in it which said "I'm a Yankee Doodle Dandy."

I passed the horses that were being groomed for the Bicentennial parade and noticed all the Disneyland characters who were mingling in and out among the excited crowds of people. I passed fathers with little kids squirming on their shoulders waiting for a glimpse of the spectacular parade.

People with sticky, Peptobismol-pink cotton candy rushed by me, and it seemed Karmel Korn was paving the street that night.

When I reached that dreaded flagpole, there stood my forlorn-looking son, his eyes looking like two burned holes in his ashen face. His shoulders drooped and the obvious strain he was under made him a pathetic sight. He looked scared. I could tell he had been crying. I wanted to reach out and hug him and tell him everything would be all right—it had never really happened—tomorrow would be a bright, shining day again.

I felt relieved that my sister and her husband had already greeted him. Bill was off trying to buy some popcorn before the parade began. Our son Barney and his friend seemed bored with having to struggle with the tourists and the congestion, but they had politely come to meet us, hoping they wouldn't have to stay for the entire night. (People who live here, near Disneyland, and come to the park every time relatives or friends come to town, sort of lose the excitement after the 100th time, and Barney would have preferred being home watching motorcycle races on TV than fighting this mob of people at Disneyland.)

The weight in my heart kept dropping into my stomach, rhythmically chanting, "Homosexual, homosexual, homosexual." My eyes locked with Larry's and I pleaded with him silently to just hang on until the relatives left tomorrow.

I wanted to pull him close to me and talk, but there was no way we could do that with all the relatives and wall-to-wall people. How could I get it across to him that he could never do anything so dreadful, or never say anything so terrible, or be anything so awful that we would not still love him? We had had twenty years of a terrific relationship—fun times, happy times.

Could that one word "homosexual" destroy all those years of joy and contentment?

I saw the hurt in his eyes. I managed a few words about how glad I was that we all got there O.K. and laughed at Bill going off in all that sea of people to find some popcorn for himself. As we stood there, waiting for the parade to pass by, my sister said she would rather see "Mr. Lincoln" than struggle with all the shoving people; so everyone except Larry left with her to see that attraction a few hundred feet away. Larry and I were alone—except, of course, for all those people and strollers in every other foot of space.

He stood there, sort of rigid, eyes dark and brooding, as if he were waiting for me to speak first. I saw the hurt in his eyes; isolation and fear were showing. We found ourselves right where the rubber meets the road. Just Larry and me. I looked in his eyes and saw tears brimming up. Then he spoke, "I'm a homosexual—maybe a bisexual."

I barely felt the crushing weight of a stroller roll over my foot and looked down to see a chubby child, too big for a stroller actually, with a grubby Yankee Doodle feather he had been chewing on. The blue dye from the feather had run and smeared all around his mouth, like a milk mustache, giving him a ghastly appearance. All this was so unreal! I welcomed the pain where the stroller had gouged my foot; it momentarily took my weary mind off the words Larry had just uttered. He said "bisexual"? What was that? The word homosexual conjured up such unknowns for me. How was I ever going to understand what all this was about?

Frantically, for I realized that the relatives would be back with us any minute, I grabbed Larry and told him that nothing mattered, but that I meant what I had said in the note I had left for him. We loved him and wanted to help him get through whatever was hurting him. I asked him to help me zip it all up until tomorrow when we could surely work out a solution.

Nothing was without a solution!

Just then Tinker Bell sailed across the sky to signal the beginning of the big celebration and all-electric parade. Why couldn't I be Tinker Bell and sail right out of this world? Why did I have to be standing there, rubbing my foot? Wasn't there some simple way of disappearing . . . resigning from the whole world? But here there was no place even to faint!

I wanted to scream or cry, but no one would have heard me anyway with kids shrieking over the excitement of the parade. Bill was still off buying his popcorn and had not returned, probably due to the throngs of people. I saw the flashes of the electric parade coming along the street, Yankee Doodle was loudly playing a flute, and all the Disney characters were marching and waving feathers and sporting even bigger feathers in their hats. Then I saw some things that looked like roosters or chickens, about twenty feet tall, each one bedecked with sparkling feathered hats. And at that point I knew I was going to throw up! But there was no place even to do that.

The noise of the machinery from the electric parade drowned out ordinary voices, and I was glad because I just sort of sobbed quietly inside for a while and no one heard me. All the focus was on the parade—Yankee Doodle, the monstrous electric chickens with the frothy feathers—and I was dying right there; but it was a quiet, suffering death, with no guarantee it would be over when the parade had passed by. I prayed between the sobs inside. Then I felt a confidence coming from deep inside me and I began to feel that if only we could resume this conversation tomorrow, I could get through tonight without cracking up. If only we could maintain something of the right relationship facade so that we didn't have to expose it all. Surely we could "put on a happy face" for the next few hours, and I could wait and die tomorrow after Janet and Mel left.

I had never before felt this consuming feeling of

shock, panic, fear and anger combined with the exhaustion I had experienced earlier in the day. But I did have enough presence of mind to step over to Larry, look him in the eyes, and tell him that no matter *what* he said he was, I loved him. I admitted to him that I felt such shock that I wasn't sure what I was thinking. I wished there were some way we could all leave Disneyland and get away from Yankee Doodle strollers, Tinker Bell and all the pink cotton candy-eating tourists. Larry and I agreed that he should leave. I would offer an excuse to the rest of the family. But before he left he let me know that if I ever told anyone else, I would never see him again.

It seemed as if hours had passed even though the encounter had lasted only a few minutes. The parade was approaching now, with fireworks shooting off and flags everywhere. About that time Bill returned, having successfully pressed his way through the crowd with his half-eaten box of popcorn. He was obviously enjoying all the festivities, not realizing that right there, where we were standing, was the site of the most shattering, emotion-packed confrontation of my entire life!

Although Larry was going to "cut out," he didn't manage to split before my sister, Janet, rejoined us at the parade route. Since she was at "Mr. Lincoln" during our encounter, she certainly didn't know what had transpired between Larry and me. But because Janet knew I'd been upset and crying, she assumed it had something to do with Larry, so she went up to him and put her hands on his shoulders. Half serious, half jokingly, she asked, "Larry, what are you trying to do, kill your mother? Hasn't she been through enough problems for a while?"

Larry looked startled, wondering how she could possibly know anything since I had not even spoken to her yet. He said he wasn't feeling well, and wanted to go home right then. His actual departure isn't clear to me, but I do remember pushing through some people after him, and telling him that I loved him and that whatever was wrong was repairable. After all, couldn't God and mothers fix everything? Broken toys, broken dishes—but how do you put a band-aid on a broken heart? Is there some magic glue you can buy that holds together fragments of a heart which is shattered beyond repair?

If you take the broken pieces and wrap them carefully in love and prayer, will they heal? How long does a broken heart stay broken? Does it need setting first before it mends?

I decided I would just have to feel amputated and bleed. Maybe if I bled long enough I would just fade away, like the noise of the parade was starting to fade away now. There must be a place to resign from the world. It isn't fair to have to continue hurting when others die and find a way out of their suffering.

I kept rubbing my foot where the stroller's sharp metal had torn the skin; that focused some attention on something besides Larry and his departure. Thank God for diversions. My heart was bleeding, but all that showed to the world was blood on my foot and a huge run in my stocking. I was glad to have something to cry about openly now—glad to have had the stroller run over my foot. Surely by tomorrow this nightmare would be over. We were at Disneyland where "dreams come true." I was awake and not dreaming. This was actually happening.

The flagpole at Disneyland was like a grave marker for me. It was where a part of me died, but there would be no funeral for me because my body was still moving around. It was my spirit, my inner being, that was buried there at the flagpole, in the magic kingdom.

2

Couldn't We Just Skip Father's Day?

Sunday was bright and sunny—Father's Day. We had all, except Larry, stayed in a motel in Anaheim, making it sort of a holiday experience. I had been so exhausted from all the hassle that I fell asleep without even explaining to Bill any of the events of the day before.

I woke up about 5 A.M. with a choking, smothering feeling and felt those deep sobs coming on again, like those of a wounded animal. There was no way out this time, except to tell Bill the whole story.

Because of his inquiring, engineering-type mind, he wanted all the facts. As I was still crying and trying to give him the details, Bill was pulling on his slacks and buttoning up his shirt, preparing to leave. "I will drive up to Covina and talk with Larry right now," he said.

Though still early, this was his way of acting out some emotion too, so he sped off. "What a way to start a Father's Day," I thought—"rushing off to drive thirty miles to confront a son about homosexuality."

Bill had been in the Navy. He was so conservative and straight in his thinking that I knew he was as ill-

24

prepared as I was to deal with this subject.

Janet and I went on to Melodyland to church, where I felt tears inching down my face all during the service. Before the service was over, Bill slipped in. I felt relieved that he had made the trip up and back, and I was anxious to know how Larry had responded to whatever Bill might have said to him. As he relayed it to me, Bill's entire attitude was that this homosexuality thing was a passing phase and Larry would grow out of it, that all kids go through stages of development. He chalked it up to sexual experimentation. Their conversation had been more general, and all in all, I am sure it relieved Larry to have Bill make the trip home to let him know we loved him and wanted to offer what help we could. But we knew so little. At this point, Bill thought AC-DC was an adaptor for a Sony plug. (A person who is AC-DC in the gay terminology can have sex with both sexes.) We were in for a lot of education, and boy, did we need it!

Bill had said, "No big thing, just a phase all kids go through; he'll grow out of this." I grabbed at his words like a comforting blanket, but inside I had this gnawing fear that he hadn't been able to accept the truth and found it easier to deny what had been discovered. He was trying to appear as if it were not such a big deal for my sake, too, thinking it would help me come out of my emotional tailspin.

We somehow got through a dinner at Knott's Berry Farm. The 24-hour period was slowly coming to an end. Saying good-bye to relatives is always sad, but this time it was particularly gripping to me since by this time Janet and Mel knew what was facing me at home. Our family background could be described as a narrow, sheltered life where roller skating to non-Christian music is about the top of the sin scale. The entire gay lifestyle and all the ramifications were completely foreign to all of us. The whole issue had been far removed from us. It was not something you discussed over dinner, that's for sure.

Mel and Janet wanted to be helpful, but they didn't know what to say. They were as angry about this sin of homosexuality as I was. We knew 1 John 1:9: "If we confess our sins, he is faithful and just to forgive us our sins, and to cleanse us from all unrighteousness." How does that work out in this kind of situation? How would it work with Larry?

I drove home alone from the airport. I really appreciated this time by myself to get in touch with my emotions and to be able to cry freely again.

Driving over a high freeway interchange, I thought how easy it would be to merely swerve the car and go over, putting an end to all these consuming thoughts about homosexuality and what I knew was ahead of me. But then I thought of all the ironing at home and all the tapes I had to send out for our ministry for bereaved families. What a mess I would be leaving for whoever came in to straighten out my affairs! So I decided to go home, do the ironing, and then maybe drive the car over a cliff later—when I had the house nice and tidy.

I once heard Phyllis Diller comment on what to do with two years of unironed laundry. "Well," she said, "if your family hasn't missed what's in the bag for that long, throw it all out." My thoughts ranged from the ridiculous to the sublime as I sped toward home.

All was quiet as I entered the house. Larry was in his room with the door shut. Thinking back, I remembered that his door had been shut frequently in recent months; but kids need privacy so no one questioned that. In fact, we had been so busy that no one had questioned him on anything in recent months, although his close friendship with a young man who sang in his group had disturbed me because they seemed so mutually dependent on each other. But he was a nice Christian boy whom Larry had led to the Lord, so I certainly couldn't balk much at him.

In order to make our talk as casual as possible, I fixed a couple of Pepsi Colas with ice and turned on some soft music. Trying to make the setting relaxed and then putting on some fresh make-up to hide the deep circles under my eyes, I knocked on Larry's door and said as brightly as I could, "Can you come out and have a Pepsi with me so we can talk about yesterday now that we are alone?" (Bill had gone on to his folks' to take a Father's Day gift and Barney was at work.)

Larry came out quietly and sat down facing me. At first the sound of the ice tinkling in the glasses was deafening. He waited for me to speak; I had hoped he would start first.

The silence was making us both apprehensive, so I fumbled for some words. "Larry, I sure don't know anything about this, but I want to know how to help. No matter what you have done, God forgives, and we love you. How can we help you? Can you help me to understand what is happening?"

This brought some genuine relief and tears from Larry, and he blurted out in short staccato phrases that he had had these homosexual feelings since he was in junior high school. He'd been so alone but now he had this friend (the one who had been spending lots of time with us), and they were in love and had been for several months.

I heard the words, but nothing fit together very well. I wanted him to talk, to express himself without my interjecting anything, but after a few minutes his voice got louder and I found myself reacting in anger at things he said. Before we knew it we both were saying wild things to each other.

I suggested that his college scholarships would be denied if the school officials knew he was homosexual. I reminded him that the director of his music group should know there were homosexuals going together on these tours, and since the director was responsible for the group, it was only fair that he be informed.

My words raced on as to how Larry's entire life would change if anyone knew he was a homosexual. I guess I really expected that Larry would immediately assess this in the same way and say he wanted to change too. The words between us flew thick and fast, and suddenly he was saying he wanted me to give him the pink slip on his Volkswagen, and that he wanted to move out immediately. He added that he wanted $500 from us right then. He said he needed it for the choral group's tour to South America.

I retorted that no way could we give him the money, particularly now, when we didn't know the direction this was going. We got into a hassle about the money. At one point, in utter frustration, he said to me, "If you won't give me the money, do you want me to hustle for it?"

I listened to that closely. The word "hustle"—didn't that mean to hurry, like "shake a leg" or "get moving"? What did he mean, "hustle" for money? Did he mean he would take money for sexual acts with men? What sort of acts? Why would he threaten that unless I gave him $500, he would "hustle"? Where had he learned terminology like that? He had been in Christian schools all his life and been involved in Christian circles! Was he telling me that he would go out and prostitute himself if we refused to give him funds?

The soft voice and gentle face I was used to seeing had become hard and fierce. Words I couldn't believe came out of Larry's mouth. "You're not my mother anymore. You are nothing to me. You will never see me again."

In responding panic I said things like, "You are emotionally ill, you need help! This is all so sick! I would rather have a son be dead than be into homosexuality!"

I made lots of emotionally charged statements which were not thought through, but they reflected my inner turmoil and desperate attempt to make him see what he was doing to his future and his life. All my caustic remarks sent him into more emotional panic and me into more tears.

I put my arms around him stating that surely we

would go to a counselor and get some help. In all these years we had been close and loving; harsh words were unknown between us. I remember him saying once that he didn't think we as parents had done anything wrong. My response was to assure him that I *had* sinned and had been forgiven, that one thing God cannot see is our sin when it is covered and cleansed away by the blood of Jesus. God's love sent His Son—the greatest detergent of all—to cleanse us from all sin.

Our conversation simmered down and I was able to see his hurts, and what he had suffered in the past. My explosion had been out of inner panic, to try and shake some sense into him. The words "hustle" and "gay lifestyle" sent me into such turmoil emotionally that I could not *respond*. I only *reacted* to them.

I thought of our spiritual friends who would react in the same shock and terror as I had if they knew Larry had this problem in his life. Reasoning with Larry, I reminded him that he was a *Christian* and that he knew what the Bible said. He had been to all the seminars for training and had an abundance of information on solid biblical teaching. I kept saying that God is able to change our lives and create new desires in us. God can cleanse us and make us whole people. Larry's eyes remained dark and sad. He stood there with a crushed expression on his face, as if he thought I was being impossible to reason with. I again burst into tears, seeing how hopeless the situation was. He had turned me off and was going to do his thing regardless of the sacrifice.

Larry turned away from me and went into his room, shutting the door quietly. I walked like a zombie back to my bedroom. I'd cried so much earlier in the day that tears were not flowing easily now. My head pounded like a hammer. Up until that time I had never had a headache or toothache in my life, but at that minute, every tooth in my head hurt, every muscle in my body felt as though it were being pulled in opposite directions. I wished I had some pills or something to help me escape for a few hours, to dull the memory of those harsh words between us.

I dug around in the medicine cabinet and found only some stale Alka-Seltzer tablets. I learned that night that if you cry long enough, and keep a pillow stuffed close to your mouth to stifle the sounds, you will ultimately become exhausted and sleep will come.

I had hoped that the pillow might suffocate me, but it didn't.

The next morning found me on the freeway driving back to Melodyland Christian Center in Anaheim, where I had heard of an outreach to people who had been homosexuals and wanted to be free from that lifestyle.

The group was called EXIT. Maybe this outreach would help me locate a mother who could tell me that everything would be all right. I needed to know that some other mother had survived this.

As I was driving to Anaheim, I asked God to comfort me in this time. I was hoping the comfort would be a warm, breathing, live mother who had been where I was and had come through the nightmare into daylight.

On the other hand, I wanted to get out of the world and stop thinking about homosexuality. Yet I knew God would give us the strength to cope with this problem. Hadn't Bill been in that near-fatal accident? Hadn't we been through death twice—losing our two older sons? Hadn't God been faithful then?

3

We're Going to Need You, Bill!

Looking back to the weekend prior to Easter vacation in 1966, I remember Bill and I had been preparing to supervise and chaperone a group of our young people who were going to spend the week at Falling Springs, a Christian resort owned by some friends from our church. Our four boys would be going along so we were anticipating a real family time.

I had just finished telephoning several of the young people, checking to see if they had their equipment and were ready for the week, and was lying on the bed checking over my own list of things to do. Suddenly, out of nowhere, I heard someone call my name! The voice sounded strangely familiar, and yet I was alone in the house. I couldn't figure out where the sound was coming from. I began to wonder if I had momentarily fallen asleep and had just dreamed that someone was calling my name.

I got up quickly, walked through the house, and as I stopped to look out the living room window I saw a tall, white-robed figure standing in the place usually occupied by our tall, leafy hedge. Then he appeared to be walking down a winding road with immense chasms on either side; debris was strewn everywhere. Walking beside him was a child, a little girl. On this rugged road he was pointing out to her the craggy cliffs and all the treacherous places along the way. I stood there transfixed, as though I were dreaming, but I felt an exuberance in my spirit that was like nothing I had ever experienced before.

This joy remained with me all through the night, and the next morning I decided to tell my pastor what had happened. "Undoubtedly the Lord is giving you this extra portion of strength to prepare you for something, Barbara." Although I welcomed his explanation, I wondered why I would need extra strength. I had a happy marriage, healthy children, a comfortable home, and secure relationships, a fun weekend ahead; what more did I need?

I couldn't imagine how his words were to be applied. I was thankful, later, that God in love throws a veil across our future so we cannot see what lies ahead for us.

The next evening I loaded our car with groceries, and with the two younger boys, Larry and Barney, started up Highway 39 to the retreat. Tim and Steve were going with the young people, and Bill had driven on ahead of us. Although the road had been washed out in many places during a recent heavy storm, to us the drive was a great adventure as we headed for Falling Springs.

Only ten miles from the resort site, without warning the headlights of the car beamed on the figure of a large man lying in the middle of the road, covered with blood. Stopping the car, I jumped out to see what I could do. The man's face was covered with blood and so distorted that he was unidentifiable, but the jacket and the trousers he wore belonged to my husband! It was Bill!

Most of the events of that night have passed from my mind because God has given me a healing from the memory of painful hours that followed, but I do remember that I managed to scramble back into the car and drive on up the mountain road to the resort to telephone for help. Fortunately the forest service had seen the headlights when Bill's car flipped over, and had already requested aid. Leaving the car and the boys at the resort, I was driven back down to the scene of the accident. By this time others coming up the road behind me had gathered around Bill. It took the ambulance over fifty minutes to thread its way up the mountain road, and then the attendants didn't seem to be in a hurry to get back down. Obviously they didn't think Bill would survive the trip down the mountain anyway.

As I rode along in the front seat of the ambulance, I remembered the vision and began to see the meaning. I was the little girl, and the Lord was showing me the treacherous road and warning me of the impending dangers. With calm assurance I directed the driver down that hazardous highway, and in twenty-five minutes we pulled into the emergency entrance of the Inter-Community Hospital in Covina.

A doctor we had known for many years met us as Bill was being transferred to a stretcher. His face registered disbelief at his first glimpse of my husband. Bill's face was so shattered, so disfigured. A gash in his head exposed a part of his brain which was glistening and throbbing, one eye lay about even with the area where his nose would normally be.

Although I had remained calm during the height of the emergency, now, as Bill was wheeled down the white corridor, I began to slowly crumble. I knew that even the removal of his clothing would be no simple task—the glass from the shattered windshield and his eyeglasses had imbedded itself into his skin and clothing.

A nurse came from the room where they had taken Bill, and handed me his wallet. She asked me to go through it for information needed for his admission. My hands shook as I fumbled through the plastic dividers, trying to locate his identification card. There in that brown wallet, worn with use, I discovered a faded picture of myself, along with a poem I had given him some time back. The paper was faded and pressed tightly together. I had no idea Bill had carried that picture of me, or the poem. Suddenly I began to weep uncontrollably—I couldn't even read the words. I slipped it into my purse and just allowed the tears to flow in a much-needed release.

Meanwhile, friends had come. In the restroom, they helped to wipe the blood off my clothing and hands where it had remained since the encounter on the mountain road. When I came out of the ladies' room, I was met by the grim faces of the attending physicians. They informed me that they had to call in a neurosurgeon to determine the extent of the brain damage and an eye specialist to try to save one eye. One doctor told me to go home and get some rest. They would talk to me about their findings in the morning.

"Brain damage," the doctor had said. How much would that affect his life? Would he be the same as before? I already knew from the surgeon that extensive surgery was necessary to replace his eye and repair the distortion of his face, but the "brain damage" phrase captured my attention.

Someone took me home that night and stayed with me, since the children had remained up at the retreat (thanks to a wise Christian counselor who knew they would be better off up there, rather than down the mountain where there was uncertainty and no definite news as yet). I sent word back to the camp that we needed their prayers, and assured them I was all right.

The next day several doctors examined Bill and came out of the room wearing heavy expressions. They told me that there had been extensive brain damage, with some nerves being sheared off. More testing would have to be done when his condition stabilized, but at this point, he couldn't be moved or even cooperate with any examinations; we just had to wait and be patient. Scripture verses about patience floated in and out of my mind: "Be strong and do not lose courage, for there is reward for your work" (2 Chron. 15:7, NASB), "You will have courage because you will have hope. You will take your time and rest in safety. You will lie down unafraid, and many will look to you for help" (Job 11:18–19, TLB). That was true. I had so much prayer support and love behind me from my family, my friends, and my church that I could rest this whole situation in God's hands and know it had come into our life through God's special filter. He was in charge of the future.

The old Bill was gone. The man lying there in the bed with his head wrapped in bandages, unable to utter a sound, was a total stranger. He was uncooperative with the nurses, angrily pulling over the huge glass containers with his injectables. Attendants had to use side rails and restraints to prevent him from hurting himself or someone else. Who was this stranger? Would he ever know who we were and be a part of the family again?

Finally, after completing some extensive tests, the specialist in charge asked me to come to his office so he could explain the prognosis to me. He asked me to be seated in a comfortable chair and tried to make me feel at ease. He offered me a cup of coffee even though he knew I didn't drink coffee. I could tell he was trying to set the scene for some shattering news.

I had four boys to raise. At this time, two were teenagers and two were under twelve years of age. I needed to know the limits and the possibilities, and wanted it all to hang out.

Diagnosis: Severe brain damage; loss of sight in one eye, with severe damage to the remaining eye.

Prognosis: Permanently and totally disabled. Recommend commitment to Sawtelle Veterans Hospital.

"You mean he will be a vegetable for the rest of his life?" I asked, in shocked disbelief.

"With the damage he sustained, it is fortunate he is even alive."

My mind couldn't absorb it all. My Bill. He had always been active, a good mechanical engineer, a Lieutenant Commander with a brilliant Naval career behind him. How could it be that he would live as a vegetable in a veterans hospital until he died?

The doctor said that all the necessary arrangements would be made so that it would be easier for me, and I would be contacted before any transfer was made.

Numbness had settled on me like a fog. I made my way out to the car and just sat there by myself, trying to reconstruct the conversation to see if possibly I had not understood what was transpiring.

I opened my purse for a handkerchief and found the little poem which I had tucked away the night of the accident, the one Bill had saved in his wallet with the picture of me.

> Not until the loom is silent and the shuttle
> ceases to fly
> Shall God unfold the canvas and reveal the
> reasons why
> The dark threads are as needful in the weaver's skillful hand
> As the threads of gold and silver in the pattern
> He has planned.

The words of the psalmist, "The Lord is my light and my salvation, whom shall I fear? The Lord is the strength of my life, of whom shall I be afraid?" (Ps. 27:1) echoed through my mind. God had promised to be my strength when Bill had none; to be my light, when Bill's vision was unable to function.

I had to learn to lean on that promise during the many months ahead. Bill was broken and shattered—physically and mentally. But doesn't our God delight in touching broken people and making them whole? Regardless of the counsel of the doctor, I decided in my heart, alone with God in the car that afternoon, that we would bring Bill home—and give God an opportunity to do a restoration in his life. Sawtelle Veterans Hospital was not the answer for Bill. He belonged at home where there was love from us, where God's love would be shown through our friends, and where God would undertake for him through a long period of healing.

Bill's first weeks at home were discouraging. Many times Bill would say to me, "Who are you? Do you work here?" One night when I was getting ready for bed he asked, "Don't I know you from someplace? Haven't I seen you before?"

I was learning lessons in patience and so was Bill. A psychologist started to work with him, helping to restore Bill's memory, step by step, by going back and planting ideas and then having Bill fill in some blank spaces.

What really tore me up emotionally was the visit we made one morning to the Society for the Blind in Los Angeles to find out whether Bill could qualify as "legally blind." After administering tests, the examining physicians said Bill was a borderline case. They discovered that one eye had some vision, although it didn't "track" or work with the other eye. Bill had to keep a patch over it, otherwise he became dizzy and had trouble keeping his balance. The other eye had a blind spot from 1:00 to 5:00 on the eye circle, which was within the range of blindness. After a long explanation, the doctors offered him a white cane and a choice of educational tapes and records which would be sent to the house. He would be notified if and when an increase in his monthly disability check was granted.

As time went by our whole family was having to make adjustments in our attitudes. Bill was a changed personality. Whereas he had been a perfectionist, and meticulous with details, he was now forgetful, unable to remember what he had done in the past, unaware of events which had transpired. It taxed all of us to cope with the changes. Actually, though, we all developed a sense of humor. We laughed when Bill would watch old movies on TV and enjoy the same ones over and over, not realizing he had seen them several times before. With the passing of time, his intense counseling sessions with the psychiatrist enabled him to associate me with someone he knew in the past; and the boys gradually came into focus as a part of his life which he had forgotten.

Then we began to see a rapid return of his memory. I could see almost daily progress. God was performing a miracle! Bill's eye, which had been almost closed since surgery, began to slowly open. After several months, the eye patch was removed and his eye began to appear close to normal. This created some mixed emotions, since the insurance company had paid him $10,000 for "complete loss of the eye." Now it was open and he was *seeing* out of it! Although both eyes were not "tracking" together, they were improving. (The insurance company stuck by their original decision, paying the claim because the eye was malfunctioning.)

Psychotherapy was a tool God was using to rebuild Bill's memory bank. Love from us in the family encouraged him to keep hanging in there. We urged him to keep on trying, to keep on improving, even if it was slow and painstaking work.

After many months of progress, Bill began working on some engineering paper work at home. Then he advanced to part-time work at the company where he worked prior to his accident. I drove him back and forth, or occasionally a friend would bring him home because he was still not able to drive. His brain damage had caused traumatic epilepsy, and for many months we learned how to help him avoid seizures by preventing stress. In time, all this became a thing of the past along with other residual problems and handicaps which resulted from his accident.

A year or so later, when the doctors at the Veterans

Administration examined Bill for continuation of his disability, they were amazed as he answered their simple questions—like, "Who is the President of the United States?" Or, "Who was the Father of our Country?" They could hardly believe he was back working part time as an engineer, when a year ago they had written on his medical chart: "Completely and totally disabled. Unable to be rehabilitated. Arrange for admission to Sawtelle Veterans Hospital for lifetime care."

They credited Bill's strong spirit and his will to get well, and they gave much of the credit to me, for patiently encouraging him in many ways. We gave the credit to the Lord for mending his broken body, for healing his fragmented memory and binding up the hurts in his mind. *God delights in touching broken people and making them whole!*

It seemed impossible when I found his bleeding body on that mountain road that today, twelve years later, Bill would be back working full time as a mechanical engineer, living proof of a miracle happening before our eyes!

The Lord knew Bill would be desperately needed in the years ahead, as blow after blow was to fall on our home, shattering our family with a devastating force, filling our cup of sorrow and suffering to overflowing. We had met this crisis and had passed the test. "With men it is impossible, but not with God: for with God all things are possible" (Mark 10:27).

4

Steve, Vietnam, and Home

Then in 1968, Steve, our handsome eighteen-year-old son, joined the U.S. Marines. The Vietnam situation was swooping up all his friends who seemed to see glory in the conflict, and Steve didn't want to be left out. In our church service the day before he left for Vietnam, we sang the gospel song, "Safe in the Arms of Jesus," and had special prayer for him.

The next day I drove Steve down to Camp Pendleton Marine Base, near San Diego, to say good bye. As he swung his green Marine overnight bag over his shoulder on that rainy March day and gave a final wave, I tearfully watched him disappear into the barracks unit. Somehow inside I felt a finality about that good-bye. Driving back home alone, with the wipers making a rhythmic, noisy pattern on the windshield, I felt the need of some company so I put on a music tape in the cassette player. As I listened to John Hall sing "The King Is Coming," my heart was blessed.

Steve's first letters from Vietnam did not reflect the anticipated glory. Instead they were full of terror, anxiety and discouragement with the futility of it all: the intense heat, the tropical bugs, the overwhelming

40

loneliness and continual fear of capture or death by the enemy. One letter said, "There is nothing a plane ticket home would not cure." His trust in God and in freedom came through in his letters, but his youthful concept of life was insufficient to accept the brutal reality of war.

On a map hanging in our kitchen we marked the places that Steve mentioned in his letters. We had a red circle around DaNang where he had been stationed for several days. Each day the Los Angeles *Times* carried a list of the boys who were killed in Vietnam, and each day the list was longer. Our troops were taking a terrific beating. That summer our losses were heavier than at any other time during the war.

I awoke one morning early in July, unable to sleep. I felt burdened to write to Steve. The two younger boys, Larry and Barney, were at a church camp in the mountains, and Tim was in the Air Force; so Bill and I were alone.

I typed out a lengthy letter, assuring Steve that he was safe in the arms of Jesus—even in Vietnam. I told him that no matter where he was or where we were, we shared the confidence that he was a Christian. Somehow it seemed imperative to remind him specifically that he was God's child and that he was precious in God's sight. It seemed vital to me to give Steve this assurance that he was *safe* with Jesus at his side. There was some humor at the end of the letter, and I, as usual, kissed my signature, leaving an imprint of pink lipstick.

We learned weeks later that Steve had received that particular letter from me on a Saturday morning. Disregarding the rule that all mail had to be burned, Steve had shoved the letter in his wallet after reading it at breakfast. That same day his entire company was wiped out by North Vietnamese bullets. Sixty-five men were killed. And Steve was found lying face down in a muddy rice paddy two days after the vicious attack.

Although he was killed on July 28, 1968, it was several days later before a black car with "U.S. Marines" printed on the side pulled up to the house. Two men dressed in Marine uniforms rang the doorbell. I knew their message before I opened the door. Steve was "Safe in the Arms of Jesus" now. No more suffering in the Vietnam heat, no more fear of capture, of torture. His turmoil and distress had ended.

About ten days elapsed before his body arrived at the mortuary in Glendora. The law says that when someone dies in a foreign country, a member of the immediate family must identify the body. Since Bill was not emotionally up to this grim task, I knew it had to be me when the mortuary called for someone to come. Because this was a once-in-a-lifetime ordeal, I reasoned that I could draw strength from the Lord to get through this one day.

Standing in that flower-filled mortuary in Glendora, looking at this large box with the hermetically-sealed glass top, I saw a body that had lain in a muddy rice paddy for two days; the swelling and bloating in the tissues was obvious. The combination of tropical weather and ten days' travel time made the identification even more difficult.

As the mortician asked me to verify with my signature that the body I was looking at was that of the person whose name appeared on the paper he was holding, I experienced in that moment a pain and isolation that was enough to last a lifetime. The large box with a sealed glass top, covering a shattered, bloated body—an official paper with Steve's name on it, along with a description of him—yes, the name did belong to the body. That part was over. The sickly, sweet smell of the flowers in the mortuary lingered with me as I stumbled out the door and into the fresh air, but God was giving me grace for that one day and it was sufficient for my need.

In accordance with Bill's desire for a memorial service that would reflect the testimony of Steven's faith in God, the congregation sang, "Safe in the Arms of Jesus," and our pastor gave a message about our loss being heaven's gain. He said, "We know God sometimes takes His precious flowers for His garden at a time in their life when they are closest to Him." From Steve's letters, we knew this to be true. The memorial service was printed so that it could be shared with other families who had lost their sons in Vietnam. That marked the beginning of a ministry of sharing God's grace with other hurting parents.

Several months after his death, a large package containing Steve's personal effects arrived at the house. Bill and I took the box into the bedroom and together we quietly went through everything. A moldy, musty odor penetrated every article, but Bill handled each one carefully. Steve's wallet was stuck together and the papers in it were difficult to separate; but shoved down in the wallet we found the long, typewritten letter from me which he had received that morning before he was killed.

Bill carefully pulled the letter out, and we reread it together and wept. It was like an echo from the past, a sign of God's love, telling us that the letter had been read by Steve and then returned to assure us of that final commitment.

Part of my letter to Steve read: "Remember the little motto in the kitchen which says, 'The clock of life is wound but once, and no one has the power to tell just where the hands will stop, at late or early hour. Place no faith in tomorrow, for the clock may then be still.' Steve, when our clock in life will stop, we don't know. I am thankful that no matter what happens, your life, even as tender in years as you are, has been committed to Christ for eternity. When our earthly body dies, our soul lives on forever, and we know that life does not end at the grave but that we have a future forever with God. Since I said good-bye to you in March, I have had an awareness that no matter what comes into our lives, our future is safe in God's hands.

We don't know what the future holds, but we know the One who holds our future. This life is so brief and fleeting. I was reading in a booklet by Billy Graham that even if a person lives to be 70 years old, that is only 25,000 days in all. And if I live to be 70, I will only have 8,000 days left. In your last letter you were counting the days until you came home, and until then we must put all our faith in Jesus to make each day count for eternity."

The letter ended with, "When you left, you told Barney to hit a home run for you—about the only homers he hits now are the front window of the house *again.*" The lipstick where I had kissed my signature had faded into the typewriter ink, making it sort of a pink blob around the closure. It was somewhat comforting to know the battle for him was over. He wasn't fighting or hurting anymore. He truly was "Safe in the Arms of Jesus" forevermore.

We had a quiet peace about Steve's passing that allowed us to share his faith. Vietnam was a long way off now, but we still read the list of names of the dead; now our purpose was to secure addresses of their families, to share Steve's memorial service, and the testimony of his life and death.

Some friends sent us this poem which brought much comfort to us. Perhaps others will find it helpful for their needs also.

GOD'S LOAN

"I'll lend to you for a little time,
A child of mine," He said,
"For you to love the while he lives
And mourn for when he's dead.

"It may be six or seven years
Or twenty-two or three,
But will you till I call him back,
Take care of him for me?

"He'll bring his charms to gladden you
And should his stay be brief,
You'll have these precious memories,
As solace for your grief.

"I cannot promise he will stay
Since all from earth return.
But there are lessons taught down there
I want this child to learn.

"I've looked this whole world over,
In my search for teachers true.
And in the crowds that throng life's land,
I have selected you.

"Now will you give him all your love
Not think the labour vain,
Nor hate me when I come to call
To take him back again?"

It seems to me I heard them say,
"Dear Lord, Thy will be done.
For all the joys thy child shall bring,
The risk of grief we'll run.

"We'll shelter him with tenderness,
We'll love him while we may,
And for the happiness we've known
Forever grateful stay.

"And should the angels call for him
Much sooner than we've planned,
We'll brave the bitter grief that comes
And try to understand."

5

Tim's Challenge

There's something so extra-special about your firstborn child, and our twenty-three-year-old Tim was frequently in my thoughts. I sensed that he was restless, almost as though he were running from something—perhaps an emptiness in his life. He had graduated recently from the Los Angeles Police Academy and, while he didn't have any earthshaking problems, Tim felt within himself the need for some kind of new challenge.

So it was in that summer of 1973 that Tim and two friends decided to take off in a little blue Volkswagen "Bug" for a summer in Alaska. Al was eager to escape the pressures of college exams; and Ron, also twenty-three, was trying to run from a more serious responsibility—a rapidly dissolving marriage.

They were off on a new adventure—to make some money and see our country's last frontier.

After nearly two weeks of hard driving and failure to find work to sustain their venture, not only was their morale deflated but so were their wallets. Even the "work wanted" ad scrawled in the dust caking the side of their VW hadn't helped.

Resigned to the fact that they'd about reached the limit of their resources, and hoping they'd have enough cash to make it home to Southern California, the three pulled into an Anchorage gas station to fill up the tank for the beginning of the long trip back home.

Little did they know that this gas stop was to change their lives. They had no way of knowing that Ted McReynolds, a resourceful school teacher who pumps gas in the summer, specialized all year round in showering people with his Christian love and concern.

Ted has the knack of being in the right place at the right time. That's where he was the day our three weary travelers pulled into the service station. Ted read the dusty printing on the side of the car: "We are Al, Tim and Ron from California. We need work." And he also read the messages in the boys' faces. He perceived that their need was much deeper than finding employment. So while their VW was being serviced, he talked to them about Jesus.

None of the young men were committed Christians. Tim, although surrounded by Christianity, remained very "ho hum" about his faith. Like many youngsters, he had waded through Sunday school, memory verses, and even attendance at a Christian day school. He had invited Christ into his life some six months prior to their trip (after talking to a friend who shared "The Four Spiritual Laws" with him), and on the following day, Tim had led Ron to make the same decision. Neither, however, had really gotten a handle on what was meant by the Christian walk, a daily fellowship experience with the living Christ.

After talking to them about Jesus, Ted invited all three boys to come home with him for dinner. They were reluctant, but accepted after Tim reminded the other two of the first rule of the road: "Never turn down a free meal!" They planned to stay one meal, but ended up staying five weeks!

The hospitality and the spiritual nourishment offered by the McReynolds met a real need in their lives.

Although Tim and Ron had made a profession of faith, they were starved spiritually for this nourishment they were receiving. Life began to take on a whole new meaning for them, and then Al, too, made a commitment of his life to Jesus.

The boys held late night rap sessions with Ted and began to share their faith with others. They joined in the fellowship at the Abbott Loop Chapel where they could sense the presence of God's love and goodness in the lives of the believers.

Ted assisted in securing construction jobs for them to earn enough money to get home. The rewards of a hard day's physical labor for a good wage, were secondary, however, when contrasted with the good things of God they were receiving.

After two months, Ron and Tim felt ready to leave for California. They were eager to see their families. Tim wrote in one of his letters to us: "This trip has been fantastic. . . . I had a chance to do a lot of 'deep thinking' about myself. . . . I get so excited about all the wonderful things—burdens lifted, peace of mind. . . . It's beautiful. . . . No more worries or cares—what can I say but *it's fabulous!!*"

And Ron wrote to his family: "I just can't explain how happy I am. . . . I cannot tell you how much my life has changed. I want to come home and explain it better. . . . I want you to receive Christ into your hearts."

When we read Tim's letters, we didn't know quite what to think. His statements came across with such emotion, such *zing!* He seemed so excited, so thrilled. I can remember telling myself, "Whatever it is, even if this lasts only for a flash—great!" I was having real trouble adjusting to this new image. Our son who left for Alaska because he had become disenchanted with his work and a bit disillusioned with life in general was the more familiar one. Although Tim said he was a Christian, I had never seen him really "plugged in," never seen him in the swim—he had merely been dog-paddling along or treading water when it came to his Christian experience.

Leaving Al in Alaska, Tim and Ron left for California, and I was thrilled when Tim called en route from the Yukon to say they were on their way. He called the evening of August 1 about supper time.

We always celebrate the first day of the month at our home—I change the sheets, try a new casserole, or we go out to a play or for dinner. I just *love* a new month. So our boys grew up enjoying this holiday spirit on the first of the month too!

Tim's voice radiated over the telephone when he asked, "What are you doing, Mom, to celebrate this new month?"

"I'm home waiting for a call from you!" I replied. "Your phone call will be my celebration, since you've called *collect,* as usual!" And we laughed.

I could hear the eagerness in his voice across those thousands of miles. Even as we talked I could sense a new closeness, a new bond of understanding building between us. Tim's voice sparkled with excitement as he anticipated telling us about the details of his experiences firsthand.

God had done so many terrific things in his life, and Tim said he knew the Lord was going to use his testimony.

How his heart was changed. I could hardly believe that my son—the one who always displayed such a placid personality—had become suddenly so vivacious and alive! He just kept on sharing, with such a child-like, refreshing faith.

I was so thrilled that as soon as Tim and I concluded our conversation, I quickly dialed my sister to tell her of Tim's enthusiastic faith. I was just overwhelmed with the change in his personality, and we rejoiced with him in the brightness of his new commitment.

And they were on the way home!

Just five hours following Tim's phone call from the

Yukon, that little blue Volkswagen had a head-on collision with a truck being driven on the wrong side of the road by a drunk driver. Tim and Ron were instantly ushered into the presence of Jesus. Only their two broken bodies remained inside the crumpled ruins.

Our immediate reaction, when we heard that the boys' lives had been snuffed out by the accident, was one of shock and anger. "It's unfair! Why would God take them now, just when they had begun sharing His love with others?"

In our confusion and anguish we only gradually became aware that God had a plan to reach others with His love—people the boys couldn't have reached if they had lived. And God left the seventeen-year-old truck driver with another opportunity to receive Jesus Christ as Lord and Savior.

I first began to feel God's hand in the events which were to follow when Ted McReynolds called from Alaska and said, "I want to come down and take part in the memorial service. Those boys were radiant when they left here. What happened to them while they were with us was tremendous, and we are not going to let their testimony die in the Yukon. We want to share the miracle of their lives back down in California with you."

With Ted's words, I began to feel a lifting of my spirit. God's plan began to unfold. It was as though He had tossed a pebble of His will into the pond of the boys' lives, and the ripples were beginning to spread. I would never have believed at the time just how far-reaching they would be.

The first touch of God's life-changing power came on the day after the accident when Ron's wife, father, mother and sister came to know Jesus for themselves. They had planned to resist Ron's evangelistic efforts, but his death had broken their resistance. Ron's desire for them to receive Christ had been fulfilled even faster than he could have imagined.

The next Sunday morning, Ron's entire family walked down the church aisle to publicly confess their faith in Christ. It's difficult to explain my feelings at that moment, for I was nearly bursting inside with the magnitude of what God was beginning to do through the death of Tim and Ron. I, who normally in my grief would be in the background seeking comfort, felt compelled to walk forward with them, wanting to share my thoughts with my fellow church members.

Our pastor tried to dissuade me. Perhaps he thought I was driven by grief and would break down. But I insisted. I was overcome by God's greatness. I just had to be a part of what God was doing. Ron's whole family had received Christ. God really *was* working all things together for good! It was impossible for me to sit on the sidelines and weep when I knew without any doubt that Tim and Ron were more alive than ever. They were rejoicing in heaven, and we were experiencing the overflow of their joy.

With no notes, but propelled by the Holy Spirit, I found myself speaking for the next ten minutes to the large congregation. My voice was calm and I was not crying. Looking into the audience I saw tears in many eyes as I said, "If this had happened a year ago, I couldn't have taken it. We had pushed Tim into involvement with church and other Christians, but he remained dry and uninterested. Many times we had even *paid* him to go to Christian conferences. He had been a part of Christianity, but it had never really been a part of him. Our greatest comfort now is that he had found reality in Christ, and that he was *so ready to go!*"

In the first few days following Tim's death, we began getting letters and phone calls from various people to whom he had written. Evidently, just two days before that fatal accident, Tim had spent the entire day writing old friends to tell them what God had done in his life. Now, even before his body had arrived from Canada, we were receiving calls from friends who said, "I just saw the newspaper article about Tim's death and only this morning I received a letter from him in the mail!"

The week quickly passed as family and friends gathered to plan the "Coronation service" and await the arrival of the boys' bodies from the Yukon Territory.

"I have never had to do this—call the same family twice to come up and identify a body killed in a foreign country," the poor mortician said. "But, Barb, would you please come up again and identify Tim's body? It arrived from Canada, and you know the governmental regulation we had to comply with before when Steve's body came back from Vietnam."

Although I experienced deep grief over the loss of my oldest son, I thank the Lord that I was not overwhelmed by my sorrow. The Lord had imparted to me an inner assurance and joy in the knowledge that somehow He was going to use the testimony of Tim's changed life to reach others for himself. I felt the grace of God wrapping around my heart. He was walking with me through this heavy, deep valley.

As I stood in that mortuary, waiting to identify Tim's broken body, I was reliving an old, bad dream. This was the very same room, the same wallpaper, the same carpeting, the same everything—except here was another box with another boy in it. So unreal! How unbelievable that this could happen to me *twice!*

I saw the shattered body and signed another paper stating that this was the right name to go with the crumpled body of my son. But God reminded me that this was not Tim. This was only his earthly shell. Tim was not there. And I began to see the glory in all this! It was as if I could look up and see Tim standing there, all bright and smiling at me, saying "Don't cry, Mother. I am here with Jesus. I am finally Home! Don't feel bad."

There had been a beautiful change in Tim's life, and there was *beginning* to be a change in me.

Most of that same congregation who had heard me speak the previous Sunday in church attended the Coronation service for Tim and Ron. We didn't call it a funeral because we were celebrating their triumphant homegoing. We didn't even refer to it as a "memorial" service. We asked the ushers and pall bearers not to wear black suits. The dresses my sister and I wore were green—a symbol of *life*. And when we picked out the clothes for Tim's body, we included a colorful tie. The entire mood reflected God's power to bring triumph out of tragedy. The music was uplifting and majestic, complete with the "Hallelujah Chorus" at the close.

As Ted McReynolds told of the fulfillment that Tim and Ron had found in their relationship with Jesus, he explained that the same joy and abundant life were available to anyone who desired them. Many attending the service responded to this gospel message, and death continued to produce life. The boys' story was just beginning its long, life-changing journey.

As a family we chose two special ways to remember Tim. First, we decided that Bill would make a tape recording of the Coronation service. Then, we compiled a "Memory Book" containing letters, pictures and little momentos which had belonged to Tim. The book has since grown to be almost nine inches thick as we have added letters from friends and others who have come to the Lord after hearing Tim's story. On the leather cover of the memory book is Tim's name; on the back, an adhesive bumper-type sticker which always thrills my heart as my thoughts turn towards memories of Tim. In large purple letters, the sticker boldly proclaims: "HEAVEN IS JUST OUT OF THIS WORLD."

The memory book and the coronation recordings have been like missionaries, reaching out to people who want answers about life and death. We had no idea that Tim and Ron's enthusiasm for Christ would thrust us into such a widespread ministry. We had made the tapes for a few interested friends, including people in Anchorage who couldn't attend the service. But since that time we have mailed out almost 3,000 tapes and brochures to people who have heard about the boys' story. It's been five years now since their deaths—and nearly every week we receive requests for more copies of the tape.

One exciting story of how the cassette tapes have been used was described in a letter which we received from Ketchikan, Alaska:

> We have had a recent tragedy of our own, and your tape has made it more bearable. A young father (28) at one of our logging camps was killed two weeks ago. He had been a Christian only 8 months, and in that time had won many to the Lord. He was very outgoing and lived life to the fullest. Dennis had heard Tim's memorial tape and had said, "That's the kind of going home service I would want!" And that's just what he had. The Lord's timing is so beautiful. He had us all prepared by your tape to accept what happened to Dennis. He gave his life for his two buddies when he saw a log coming and pushed his friends out of the way. He had just led one fellow to Christ minutes before the accident. They both were injured and Dennis was killed instantly. His wife was able to come in from camp, go to the hospital and pray with and comfort both survivors. I have never seen God so anoint a person with love and compassion. It had to be Jesus.

Immediately after we were informed of Tim's accident, a blanket of friends and relatives seemed to surround us. But as time passed, I felt I needed something else—something more of *Tim* to hold onto.

One day while going through some old Christmas cards, I came across a letter Tim had written to me when he was still in training at the Police Academy. In the letter, he told about his concern for the shattered lives he saw all around him. "I'd be willing to sacrifice anything to see these people come to the Lord," he wrote.

I'm sure Tim never dreamed how great that sacrifice would be, but what a blessing at the same time. As we shared his story, the memory book and the coronation tape with those he left behind, many came to know Christ.

But the loneliness began to creep slowly back into my life, especially as the Christmas season approached. Five months had passed since the accident, but I often became discouraged.

I really felt cheated that I'd never heard Tim's testimony in his own words before he died. I kept wondering why no one at the church in Alaska had taped the service that evening when Tim and Ron had told their story and then were baptized. Over the past several months, I had even written to several people in that church, asking if a tape had been made but each time the answer was negative.

On December 12, the day before my birthday, I wasn't too surprised to find a small package in the day's mail. As I opened the tiny parcel, wrapped in brown paper, I found a very worn-looking cassette tape. The edges were chipped, and it appeared to have been used many times, over and over. There was no label, no note, no return address, just this tape with the Anchorage, Alaska, postmark on the outside.

I put the mystery tape on my cassette player and heard *Tim's own voice speaking to me!* It was like Hebrews 11:4: "He being dead, yet speaketh."

My name is Tim Johnson, and I'm third in the group that came up from California. Funny, we were headed for South America. I don't know how we got here, but . . . uh . . . the Lord works in miraculous ways. Praise the Lord! I'm glad He did. I had a good job in Los Angeles. I don't know why I quit. It must have been from the Lord.

Like I say, we were in Alaska and I met Ted, thanks be to God. And, as he can vouch for me, I've been pretty miserable since I've been up here. Especially these last couple days. I was brought up in a Christian home and Christian schools, but after graduation I departed and went my own way. It wasn't until last December that a friend sat down with me and showed me the real way to the Lord—the *true* way. I was on fire for a couple of months, and then I just fell by the wayside. It wasn't until I came to Alaska that things really started happening in my life. For instance, this morning I was filled with the Holy Spirit, and . . . uh . . . since then it's just been . . . I dunno . . . I have a smile on my face. And everyone looks at me like I must have been a sour lemon before. But now it's just different, and I'm thankful that I'm here today. Thanks be to God.

And then I heard the splashing of the water as he was baptized, and the music and the singing, "The Joy of the Lord is my strength" and Tim's voice as he came up out of the water saying, "Praise the Lord!"

God's love was reaching out to me! Receiving that tape of Tim's testimony in the morning mail was like a sparkling diamond from God. I was overwhelmed with His goodness, and was greatly comforted. What a birthday present for me! Suddenly Tim was right there with me again. The mystery tape had become my *miracle* tape!

The ripples made by Tim's death have spread far, touching many lives. I still feel the ache of Tim's passing, and tears come easily in spite of our rejoicing at his homegoing. But I'm so grateful that God allowed me to see that when Tim stepped through the doorway of death, he was just beginning to live. When that doorway opened, there was a shaft of brightness and warmth that drew many people into a closer relationship with God and an eternal friendship with Jesus Christ.

SAFELY HOME!

I am home in Heaven, dear ones;
All's so happy, all's so bright!
There's perfect joy and beauty
In this everlasting light.

All the pain and grief are over,
Every restless tossing passed;
I am now at peace forever,
Safely home in Heaven at last.

Did you wonder I so calmly
Trod the Valley of the Shade?
Oh! but Jesus' love illumined
Every dark and fearful glade.

And He came Himself to meet me
In that way so hard to tread;
And with Jesus' arm to lean on,
Could I have one doubt or dread?

Then you must not grieve so sorely,
For I love you dearly still;
Try to look beyond earth's shadows,
Pray to trust our Father's will.

There is work still waiting for you,
So you must not idle stand;
Do your work while life remaineth
You shall rest in Jesus' land.

When that work is all complete,
He will gently call you home;
Oh, the rapture of the meeting!
Oh, the joy to see you come!

—Anonymous

6

Where Have All the Mothers Gone?

My friend, you wore your Jesus like an iron-on
   patch,
But He could not cover the holes in your shabby
   coat.
Yet when you laid aside that threadbare rag
And laughed with me, and wept with me, and sim-
   ply loved me,
I saw His love in you.
And you wore a shining robe which drew me to His
   side.*

—Eleanor Whitesides

Driving toward Melodyland and thinking about
Larry's problem, I tried to focus on logical questions to
ask, but I was having trouble coming off the panic button and out of the emotional fog which had enveloped
me for the past thirty-six hours. You know the game
that has a rubber ball attached to a rubber band on a
wooden paddle? Tormenting thoughts would be batted
out of my mind by the paddle for a minute, and I would

---

*Taken from *His* magazine, February, 1978.

get some other idea circulating, and then *bang!*—the ball was back slapping the paddle again. As the ball hit, it would say, "Homosexual," and the consuming ugly thought would travel around and around in my mind. No matter how much I tried to concentrate on Philippians 4:8—"Finally brethren, whatsoever things are true, whatsoever things are honest, whatsoever things are just, whatsoever things are pure, whatsoever things are lovely, whatsoever things are of good report; if there be any virtue, and if there be any praise, think on these things"—the sordid, monstrous word "homosexual" would flood back at me with all its persistence.

At the Center, I talked briefly with a young man who had come out of a homosexual background. But I was still looking for a *mother* to talk to. Couldn't he refer me to any mothers who had come through this, who could give me some hope? He knew of no other mothers with whom I could talk. If there are twenty million homosexuals in the world, as the statistics say, how come I cannot find one mother to talk to me? Are they all in the "Home for the Bewildered"? Do they all die an early death or commit suicide? The young man admitted that his own mother did not know of his homosexual involvement in the past, so she would be of no help. Everything else he said to me was a blur, because I wanted so much to have a mother's consolation. I surely couldn't get help from a kid, an ex-homosexual. How could he understand my fears? My anguish? My shattered heart? If his own mother didn't even know about him, how could he help me in my isolation?

As I headed back to Covina, I vowed that if I ever *lived* through this situation, I would be available to help other mothers going through this pain. I would learn and grow and get the answers—perhaps initiate a caring unit for parents who are suffering as I was. I thought of the song, "Where have all the flowers gone?" Only I kept thinking, "Where have all the mothers gone?" Surely there had to be *one* around who had survived this pain and would help me. *I am so alone. Isn't there someone who can tell me what to do, where to go for help? How do I cope with the feelings which overwhelmed me yesterday and are choking me today? They range from extreme anger at myself and Larry, to an intense love which seems to wash over me and wants to include him and every other person who has the label of homosexual. Self-pity, guilt, frustration, isolation—this is what I am feeling. What is Larry feeling? He was so gentle and kind. Now he has become someone I don't know.*

As I approached the house, a heavy sense of apprehension flooded over me. When I opened the door I immediately noticed that Larry's favorite tan and brown afghan was not in its usual place on the sofa. Several familiar things were missing from the living room. Stumbling down the hall to Larry's room, I opened the door and found it completely empty. Larry was gone.

During those few hours I was in Anaheim seeking counseling, he had packed his things and vanished into thin air. I couldn't believe he had cleaned everything out in such a short time. A beat-up Peanuts poster was still nailed to the wall which said, "I have tried long enough to understand others, now let them start understanding me."

Why did he leave the poster? Perhaps he had just forgotten it in his rush to escape before I returned home. Did it have some special meaning, showing us his hostility because we didn't understand? Perhaps he left it up thinking it would leave a big hole in the wall if he removed it. I wonder if he considered the big hole he left in our hearts.

In the short span of two days, our lives were completely upside down. My husband insisted it was a phase that Larry would outgrow. Our son Barney, who was seventeen, was so busy repairing dirt bikes in the garage that he paid little attention to the departure of his brother. He did show some concern that I had been crying for two days solid, and asked me if Bill and I were having trouble. So rather than have him think that, I confided to him that Larry was having a problem with his sexual identity. I could hardly utter the word "homosexual" at that point. Barney didn't seem too disturbed, but went on quietly working on motorcycle repairs. He evidently knew more about the whole situation than I did, but figured he'd be more helpful by going along in his own quiet way than by adding fuel to the already inflamed emotional scene. Barney had a quiet, unruffled manner which seldom showed much unrest, but he did give me a few extra hugs that week and showed he really cared by his thoughtful ways.

We had to do something about that room. We could not have a huge empty space just staring at us. I went in there again and saw some old tennis shoes Larry had left in the closet and an old puppet he had played with as a child. I decided to shut the door and pretend he was on a long trip. Little did I know then that I was the one going on the long trip. By keeping the door shut, I reasoned with myself, I wouldn't be reminded of his absence and my torn-up emotions might heal.

Waves of pain and nausea hit me when I went into the bathroom which joined Larry's room with Barney's. The toothbrush holder had one lone toothbrush in it. Thinking back to that toothbrush rack which held four brushes only a few years ago was devastating. Now two of the boys were in the grave, and the third one was out there somewhere. The fourth boy was whistling in the garage as he worked on his dirt bike. "Maybe," I thought, "I will buy three new toothbrushes and stick them in the holder—it wouldn't be so lonely then."

Another day went by. Food was sticking in my trachea. Sleep would not come unless I cried for hours and was exhausted from grief. This was worse than death. At least then, we had friends around who cared. The house had been filled with flowers and people; food was sent in—thoughtful gestures reminded us of their love and God's love. But this was a living hell! There was no one I could tell. How do you explain the disappearance of a son? How can you explain homosexuality when you don't understand it yourself? In bereavement people stick together and healing comes, but in this circumstance each person involved stands alone. I blamed myself; my husband kept insisting it was a passing phase; and although Barney was quiet about his feelings, the strain was obviously there.

I felt trapped, betrayed and frightened. I longed to share the guilt, anger, self-pity with someone else who would understand. I wondered if I was going insane because I didn't know anyone else who had experienced these feelings. Inside I was torn and felt waves of fear flooding me. The isolation of being cut off from the relationship with Larry left me ripped, wounded and bleeding with burning mental pain inside. It would, in fact, have been easier to lose my mind. After all, I had such an accumulation of pain from experiences in the past that I had passed the level where people stop absorbing shock and just "go under the load."

Are there instructions someplace on how and where to lose your mind and some corresponding hints on where to find it once it is gone? Somehow these weird fragments of thought flitted through my mind and were mixed with more rational thoughts of having to fix a meal soon.

I had worked my way through grief, losing Steve and Tim in death, and was honestly able to see God's glory and plan in it. But this was completely different. There was no way to put on a Pollyanna attitude and wear rose-colored glasses. I had to realize this situation was more isolated than grief. I could go through it or I could *grow* through it. I know that one does not reach the "promised land" without first wandering through the wilderness; but at this point, I didn't want to wander—I just wanted to die. "I am tired of working my way through grief situations," I thought to myself. *I am tired of counseling others as to how Romans 8:28 works, and how all things come through God's love filter. I am tired of that filter . . . tired of the wilderness . . . tired of the nasty now and now. I want the sweet bye and bye.*

This was in June of 1975. Tim had died less than two years before; healing had taken place. Did I have to start that process again with the sweat and tears and agony of adapting to the loss, endeavoring to fill the void created by it? I had lost a son, yet he was not in a grave—he was out there *someplace.* He was gone, yet he was my own son—living, breathing, moving around in a market or driving on the freeway, yet not wanting us to know where he was.

Lines from a poem I learned in college came to my mind:

> I wish that there were some wonderful place
> called the Land of Beginning again
> where all our mistakes and all our heartaches
> and all of our poor selfish grief
> could be dropped like a shabby old coat at the door
> and never be put on again.

Would I do the same things over if I had the opportunity? I had made so many messes in my life, but God had forgiven me and given me a clean slate. Why did I have to whip myself now and feel that I was such a failure because Larry was a homosexual?

I had often heard that people sometimes just couldn't cope with life, that they came apart at the seams. Was the shattered feeling I had inside an indication that I was falling apart? Was this a sign that I'd had it? What about the question of suicide? It can be only a question because it is not really an answer, is it?

I've always thought suicide was absurd. It is like

leaving the Miss America contest after the initial run-offs because Miss California didn't get in the top ten. It is like walking out of the opera during the overture just because the conductor dropped his baton. It could never be the answer for me.

I felt as if a box were suffocating me. I was alone and couldn't even pray. All the scripture verses I had learned in my life floated through my mind. Their fragments washed through my thoughts—comforting verses about God being with me, not forsaking me. Yet I felt amputated, as if my legs had been sawed off and I was slowly bleeding to death. Hopefully the bleeding would stop soon and the pain would end. I would be out of this dream, out of this anguish. Maybe there was a land of beginning again, where we could go back to where we were before we knew about Larry, back to the beginning—a place where all our mistakes and all our heartaches could be "dropped like a shabby old coat at the door and never put on again." Right now I wanted me to be put by the door and never have to get up again.

It had been four days since the stroller with the chubby kid in it had rolled over my foot. Unthinking, I proceeded to remove the newly formed scab. It was healing fine until I pulled the scab off! I asked myself, "How come I am still raw and bleeding inside when my foot is healing easily?" I watched the blood ooze from the scabbed-over area and wondered how much blood I had to lose before I would just bleed to death. I had to face it. There was no way out except to live.

7

Survival Notes: One

June 20, 1975: A week has gone by since I have been smothering in this box. I have been in bed most of the time. No one has made any demands of me; it's almost as if I can escape from the world and live inside my own walls. Bill always said I was the spark plug around here. I really have gone dead on him now, but he has been steady, doing his job. He brings me juice, treating me as if I have the flu. The house is a mess, I am sure. I told Bill to dig up a couple get-well cards and sign a name to them and put them on the mantel. That way, if anyone came over they would assume I've been sick and unable to clean the place. If people call on the phone he says I haven't been well due to the hot weather and the flu. The fact that our house is air-conditioned and that the flu season is not in June didn't matter to Bill. On the outside he seems like the Rock of Gibraltar, but inside I know he is more like a rock of Jell-O!

There is no way to resign from this . . . suicide is out and I am afraid whatever I might try wouldn't work and I'd be back with this dreary ironing again. God is alive and working, but I feel as if I am in this tight box with the lid coming down, and no one can get to me. There has to be a way out of this. The Bible says

God will never leave us alone. He will never forsake us. I have prayed for the Lord to come and take us all away.

Nothing has happened. I am too tired to carry on my responsibilities, too exhausted from crying to talk to anyone.

Something has to happen to make me want to get out of this depression. After all, wasn't I the one people came to when they felt down? Coming here to my home and sharing had helped them out of their heaviness. Where can I go and tell someone my son is a homosexual? And that he had disappeared?

What about the hustling business he had mentioned? It didn't mean hurry, but why would he speak of it as he did—like a threat? It would be easier to go to a cemetery and place flowers on his grave than to realize we might never see him again. Could he cut himself off from us and live his new life as if he were not our son? Was this dreadful thing called homosexuality able to disrupt a family like this? *I had to learn . . . I had to find out . . . I had to get out of this box! Frantically grappling for knowledge, I had an obsessive need and desire to discover what I could about this unknown world with its vocabulary that was so foreign to me.*

I will keep writing down my thoughts each day That will help me see where I am coming from and where I'm going. I have no one to talk to, so putting things down on paper helps me know this is real—this is not. The pain is real. I have to peel myself off the wall and glue myself together. I have "to work as if it all depends on me, and pray as if it all depends on God." There is no one around to help me. God has given me strength to *want* to get out of this box. This is the first small step in getting free of the blackness I am in.

I used to work at a Christian counseling center where people came from all over for help. At that time I had no big problems, so I was detached from theirs.

Dr. Wells, whom I worked for, knows our family and Larry. I will call him and be a counselee myself. He will help me put some order in my thinking. THE WORD HOMOSEXUAL CONTINUES TO GO ROUND AND ROUND IN MY HEAD LIKE A NEEDLE STUCK ON A RECORD. When I wake up it is going, when I go to bed it is going. I move around the house like a zombie. I feel as if I have a concrete mind—permanently set and all mixed up with that one word.

Survival notes—that is what I will call these. I am going to survive. I cannot allow the sin of one child to disturb my entire family. I will find out what this is all about and how to understand it—how to understand myself. How can one word like homosexual send waves of pain and nausea over me? I have survived death, accidents, heartbreak—why is this so different? Surely Dr. Wells can give me some answers for the questions swirling around in my tired, emotional thinking process.

June 22: Dr. Wells encouraged me to take notes on our sessions together and read them over later. He knew my thoughts were so fragmented that most of the session was passing right over me. Hopefully my scribbled notes would mean more to me later. My name should be A.T. and T.—for always talking and talking. I asked him if I was losing my mind, and he assured me that as long as I kept talking I was going to be okay. I wanted a definite yes or a no, but he answered by saying that it is when people cannot talk about their problems that they get sick.

Talking is therapy; it is also costly. But at this point, I would sell all the gold in my teeth to pay for sessions with Dr. Wells because they are giving me the first relief I've had for a week.

I look forward to seeing him each session. Dr. Wells says Larry is so full of guilt and shame he wouldn't read or listen to anything at this point. We just have to let him go and pray for him. The feelings of choking and suffocation which I am having are normal anxiety symptoms, he says. That accounts for the concrete in my head, the nausea, chest pain and the feeling of total unreality. How nice to know that there are two words which explain away what I thought was the end of my rope.

Dr. Wells said we should thank the Lord for allowing us to suffer. Perhaps someday we can help some other parents—might volunteer on a hotline to help mothers survive this. At this time he knows of no other mothers who could help me. He did say that I had a gift of humor which would help me. I knew I once had it but thought it died at the flagpole at Disneyland.

O Lord, give me back my gift of humor if it will help me get through these next months without losing my sanity.

I managed a weak smile when I told Dr. Wells that another symptom I had was that my teeth itched! Funny way to describe it, but I felt as if he had explained away all my other physical manifestations of anxiety—so what about having itchy teeth? That too is attributable to anxiety, he explained.

So it was with a more quiet spirit that I came home, glad to know there was a name for my sickness: anxiety symptoms. But I have so many aches and pains today that if a new one appeared, it would be at least two weeks before I could worry about it!

I need my gift of humor so much, Lord. Will you revive it, or fix it so it works again? I am so tired of tears.

June 23: Dr. Wells says that the deceit and smokescreen made Larry change from a normal bubbly son into a stranger. He assured me that the humor inside me was like a percolating joy that would surface when it was the darkest. Oh, wow! But everything has been so black now for two weeks and it hasn't surfaced yet. Will I ever laugh again?

There is no literature for parents. No one to talk

to. Dr. Wells is all I have, and he costs so much that I can see him for only an hour or so every few days.

He paints such a depressing picture. He tells me I am not on a mother level to Larry now. I am his friend. (Long-lost friend since Larry is gone, and I am just a memory, really.) Larry is an adult man and I am an adult woman. I am no longer responsible for his choices. I can take no credit for his choices. Who wants the credit for such a choice as homosexuality? I wondered why Dr. Wells used the word *credit*. The father of the prodigal son had to let his son go and do his thing. We have to let Larry go (he is already gone—so no big choice!). Larry has to discharge his anger. I never did learn what he is so angry about, but Dr. Wells says until he discharges and acts out his anger, he will be too hostile to hear anything we would say to him. He says Larry is paranoid about others knowing of his situation, and that we must let him be angry to help him discharge his emotions. He told me to read *The Angry Book* by Dr. Theodore Isaac Rubin, which he said would help me to understand ventilation of anger.

He said if Larry did call, for me to not be readily available to him—that I should not try to satisfy all his wants immediately. Larry is very dependent, Dr. Wells said. He had observed that Larry is seldom isolated from people and always gets response and attention when others are around. Larry's quick way of getting things, his sparkling way of getting close to people are all symptoms.

I have such a cluster of emotions right now—loving Larry, hating Larry, wanting to kill him, wanting to kill myself, wanting to love him and tell him it is O.K., wanting to bury him, wanting to bury myself.

How I want to go back to two weeks ago and remember how happy life was before that Saturday when I found the books. Is Larry hurting? Is he missing the comfort of his secure home and family? How will he live? Even if he doesn't miss us, wouldn't he miss his fluffy brown dog?

June 24: I am supposed to think about how I would treat another adult who has this problem—treat Larry as if he were another adult friend. He has to make his own choices.

Dr. Wells says not to go back and say this or that caused the problem. Many things might have contributed to Larry's homosexuality. All of us have traumas which affect our personality, *but the choices are our own*. This is helpful. I will memorize that line and keep saying it over when the self-blame becomes intense and attempts to swallow me up again.

Dr. Wells says we cannot let the devil get a foothold in what the Lord has done in our family.

Steve and Tim are deposits in heaven for us. Where is Larry? The numbness and unreality of this makes me want to think I am dreaming. I'm so sick to my stomach. I could not be pregnant. Praise the Lord, I am not pregnant! I must find something in this ugly mess to be thankful for. Imagine having to change diapers with this chest pain and nausea. Making formula with bifocals would be the living end—*no way!*

I told Dr. Wells today I am thankful for two things—really had to search for them—losing ten pounds in the past week, and I'm thankful that I am not pregnant. I notice the nausea most when I brush my teeth and happen to touch my tongue on the brush—almost gags me to death. Will this wave of nausea ever go away? Will I ever be able to breathe again without this choking feeling?

Will I always feel as if I have a sack over my head? I remember when I used to work at the counseling center, a young man would come in for his session wearing a large grocery sack on his head. He graduated after many months to a large floppy hat which hung down over his face.

Thinking of situations like that sort of keeps me in touch with myself or something—at least I remember his name was Mario, and I wonder whether he had a new sack each time he came in, or did he wear the same old sack? Pondering such things can help keep your mind from thinking about swallowing razor blades.

It was smoggy today. I wonder if this is the same smog we had before the rain washed it all away last week. Or is it new smog? Just contemplating that kept my mind off Larry for the trip back home from Dr. Wells' office.

June 27: Perhaps the reason Larry admitted to me he was homosexual while we were at Disneyland was so I couldn't cry or faint or hit him. After all, with a huge Fantasy parade passing by, fireworks blazing, and wall-to-wall people, fainting or being emotional was impossible.

More than two weeks have gone by. I don't feel much better. The bleeding in my heart has stopped somewhat. The weirdness of it all seems heavier to me now. Dr. Wells keeps painting a black, black picture. Why does he make it so black?

He says I have not accepted it yet. I want to die and wish everyone would die, but that is not accepting reality. Pulling my soft afghan over me is not accepting it. What is? I feel as if I could make a fortune renting my head out as a balloon—the crying makes it feel bigger than a melon.

June 28: If only Larry were involved in a normal type sin—like being with a girl, etc. A friend called me, all hysterical, because her daughter was going off to live with her boyfriend without getting married. I wanted to tell her to be thankful. What if she were going off with another girl to live as a homosexual? But I knew that would blow her fragile personality apart, so I tried to empathize with her. However, I thought, "Oh, wow! If only she knew what I was going through, she would think her problem was small by comparison!"

Sometimes sitting down and typing out what Dr.

Wells and I talk about helps me reinforce it in my mind.

He says there is a paranoia in homosexuality—a fear of being found out. That is why Larry covered his tracks so well. I was an obstacle and a threat to him, because of all my years of doing medical investigations; he knew I could get any information I needed, on any subject. It probably shocked him that I hadn't caught him sooner.

But I had completely trusted him and never played the game of "Family Bureau of Investigation" like some mothers project on their kids. I had never checked his mail or gone through his room except to pick up laundry or deposit clean clothes. I had idealized Larry as the fair-haired son with all the spiritual depth, all the training, all the answers. We looked on him as a spiritual giant, idealizing him because he was so mature (so it seemed).

This is not a heart attack, but I wish it were. How simple to have one big pain and be out of this pressure. Dr. Wells says we are to be helpless if Larry calls. If he asks for money, I am to say, "It's scary to be broke, isn't it?" Or, "It's really tough not to know where the next buck is coming from." He says Larry has had an emotional arrest; inside he feels depressed and lost, does not know who he is, is confused in his sex role. I have idealized him and let him be the stronger one by making him become like a parent. His heterosexual line is not clear to him. I cannot control him because he has become like a parent to me. I allowed him to have more control over me than I did over him.

8

Survival Notes: Two

June 30: Dr. Wells says Larry was very dependent upon me emotionally. He says that if he is wounded or hurt badly, then he may seek help. I could go find him and shoot him, but then *I* would need help!

Things have to get worse before he can get better. All this is so unreal! Such a riddle. I'd like to go out and sit in the rocker on the porch and hold my little Mrs. Beasley doll which the kids gave me some years ago and pull her string. She'd talk to me.

There must be a way out of this. I wonder if I were placed in a mental hospital whether I'd be sent to the room where they make the raffia baskets or in the room where they take them apart. They do that, you know. With my luck, I would have to make things with yarn and that always makes my teeth itch.

I remember my mittens being crushed with ice and snow when I was little, and trying to pull them off with my teeth. That always made them itch too. Just the thought of those mittens with their wooly, icy texture gives me shivers. If only there were some diagnosis for people with itchy teeth!

July 1: A new month. How nice—ordinarily. Dr. Wells is trying so hard to paint a black picture and have me accept it. I am usually so optimistic and to have to accept the enormity and the gross realities of confronting the problem of homosexuality is just so *hard*.

Other mothers cave in and come unglued because they won't face the black picture. They prefer to think it will pass away, and they won't accept the viciousness of it.

I heard about a little boy recently who was told to draw a picture of what he thought about church. He colored the entire picture completely black with one little white square in the middle. When the teacher looked at it, she asked him what the white square was, and he said, "That's the way to get out of there!"

I told Dr. Wells that all he talked about was this black picture of homosexuality and there wasn't even a little white square to get out. Just a black picture, nothing but blackness.

Dr. Wells says that curbing or suppressing homosexuality is the best we can hope for. Doesn't God do what man cannot? How come this psychologist doesn't have any real successes in this area? Can't God put a new man in the suit? Can't God create a new heart, a clean heart? Dr. Wells says Larry is more whole now that he has told us. He doesn't have to live a double life now—he is not as fragmented (I think I'm the one who is fragmented now). How come Larry has the problem, and I am the one paying for psychological help—for me!

Dr. Wells feels Larry is a responsible person and has tremendous inner qualities which will surface—the integrity has always been the real Larry. Yet Larry didn't tell us anything about his problem until it was flushed out.

Finding the magazines and letters only brought the discovery on earlier. Again, our learning that he had a rented post office box caused him real panic. The fact that we know has taken the pressure off him now. If the pressure is off him, then where is he? Why hasn't he come back home?

July 2: I dug out a copy of the *Advocate,* a magazine for homosexuals that is sold on newsstands. Dr. Wells says reading through some of that stuff may help reduce my homophobia about all this. That word means "fear of homosexuality." And because homosexuality is so unknown to me, I have a bad case, he says. Reading that is like going through a garbage pail to get something to eat, but I've tried to choke through a couple pages. I don't understand the terminology— chickenhawk, AC-DC, and most of the codes seem like a foreign language to me. There must be another way to reduce my homophobia. I need to brush my teeth and gargle and take a bath after looking at the junk in that magazine. Can't we recognize garbage without having to taste it and smell it? I failed the experiment, threw away the *Advocate,* and decided I would find a better way to break down my homophobia.

July 3: Dr. Wells says Larry will be terribly hurt when his lover leaves him for someone else, which eventually happens. The pain will be so intense it will send him for help. I wish I knew how to pray more sensibly. Praying for the Lord to come would seem best of all. I heard Roger McDuff sing, "Come on down, Lord Jesus, and take us away . . . Let this be the day." And I thought, "Oh, yes, Lord, let it be yesterday." I have so much ironing to do and would hate to leave it all undone. See what useless thoughts are running through my head? Surely I must be on the rocky road to someplace. I wonder if there actually is a "Home for the Bewildered" or maybe I could start one. How bewildered would one have to be to qualify for checking in?

July 5: Dr. Wells says over and over that homosexuality is based on paranoia. He repeats that a lot, probably because things don't register with me. I don't catch the ball on the first bounce like I used to. In fact, sometimes I don't even know the ball is bouncing. Dr. Wells says the furtiveness, the hiding, the shame of always being rejected, blackmailed or found out, and the separation from the family is part of the paranoia. I only know I had a wonderful loving Christian son who lived here for twenty years and was a bright spot in this home. Where did he go? Who is this sullen, rebellious son with dark eyes and no light in his face—no light in his eyes? Will the old Larry ever be back?

I repeat over again to myself, "Will the real Larry please stand up?" like they do on the TV program. And always I think, "I don't know which the real one is anymore."

Dr. Wells is going away for a week to a convention. How will I manage with only *God* for a whole week? I want someone with skin on his face—someone with a strong arm to steady me as I limp in and out of the office for a therapy session.

Dr. Wells keeps telling me that we must hope Larry will get hurt badly and seek help or make him suffer in order to find help. It all confuses me so much. Larry is long gone, no one knows where, and here I am grieving over him and trying to hope he will hurt badly and go some place for help. I wonder if women who drink can endure this pain better than total abstainers like me.

July 10: Dr. Wells says that homosexuals will go through twenty hours of hell to have one hour of ecstasy, that their desire is about one hundred times as intense as normal sexual feelings. Then they ask themselves why they are suffering through all this, living in such hell, for a short time—but they are completely consumed by their homosexual desires. I know the word consumed because I have been consumed by homosexuality as a word, not an action; so in all these weeks I finally know what it is to have a word completely consume one's mind.

I was in the market today looking over the soups to see if anything looks exciting and when I saw "consomme," I thought it said "consume"! So you see everything revolves in my mind around homosexuality—even labels on Campbell's soup cans. When will this nausea pass? In pregnancy it lasts only a few months and then the heartburn begins. Nine months one can take, but this could last forever. How come no one is around to tell me when my anxiety symptoms will pass? Doesn't the Bible say to "be anxious for nothing"? I believe that, or I *used to* before this happened in my life. Is this different from other anxieties?

I cannot find anything written about Christians who get into homosexuality. Who knows? This homosexual situation has so consumed me that I wake up with it, have it all day, go to sleep with it and then start over the next day.

I am not even sure what they *do*—homosexuals, I mean. Actually, I am almost as ignorant as when I first learned about it. I know it is not sex at home alone, though. That is some progress. And bisexuality is not sex twice a month.

July 11: I am shocked that there is no information for parents on how to *survive* this trauma. I visited a large bookstore today and found fifty-eight books on "alternate lifestyles" with instructions on gay living, gay sex, gay bars, catalogs of homosexual eating places and vacation resorts for gay people; but not one book to help parents of gays know how to help themselves. There were books on survival in death; in trauma, such as becoming paralyzed or going blind; but no books for practical ways to keep on living when your chest turns to concrete and your teeth itch continually. Maybe they have some books for parents but keep them hidden away from the regular bookshelves. I didn't want to ask specifically today; I wanted the salesperson to think I was a teacher doing some research on homosexuality. When the salesperson directed me to the section on "alternate lifestyles," I tried to pretend that I was nonchalantly looking for just any old book; but the shock on my face must have registered to the top of the meter as I pulled out a couple books—and the pictures on the jackets just about did me in.

78

July 12: This has been a horrible week. It is Thursday and I feel like I am drowning in this grief.

July 13: I am still drowning. I cannot even write down how I feel today.

July 14: Saturday. I am choking now and drowning.

July 15: Sunday. O God, I can't even drag myself to church today. Could you please make a house call? And hurry!

July 16: A pastor in Pomona called to ask me to talk with a mother who had lost her son in a tragic accident. It has been many weeks since I tried to minister to anyone. After all, when you are drowning yourself, you are not in a position to help someone else swim.

I went to the house to see the family and then went with them to the funeral since family members were few. Actually she was quite alone in her grief. I wanted to tell her there are worse things than death, but she wouldn't have understood right then.

I had prepared myself to zip up Larry's situation, unzip the glory of Tim's story and share with this lady the comfort God had given me when Tim had been killed.

The funeral was comforting and serene. The mother loved the Lord and the son was a fine Christian. It seemed like a peaceful interlude for me to be sitting there. For the first time in many weeks I could weep, along with the family, and no one questioned my tears. I could drink in the words to the music and allow the scriptures to minister to me. I looked at that casket and suddenly I thought how nice it would be if I were lying there in all that soft satin comfort—all still and no more nausea or concrete-chest symptoms. I wondered if Larry would come and grieve if I died. I guess the feeling of wanting to die passes, but that must be when you are on the way out of this. And I am not out of it, by that criteria. To go to a funeral and want to exchange places with the corpse surely is not healthy thinking. It is *my* mind that is going down the tubes.

Doesn't Dr. James Dobson, the well-known psychologist, say something about there being such a short span when we are between youth and old age? He says by the time our *face* clears up, our *mind* gets fuzzy. . . .

Will I ever be able to think of anything else besides homosexuality and death? I know I am alive—I'm breathing. Why can't I get a grip on myself and realize that I have wasted enough time down in this well or pit or whatever? It certainly is not a grave, though I wish it were; and it is time now to start back in the land of the living.

July 17: I found an old shoe box today and pasted some funny paper on it and decided to make myself a "Joy Box." There is no joy here, so I will have to manufacture my own. I found some cartoons and verses and a couple poems to put in my box.

I found one cartoon that shows a lady in front of a travel bureau. She is saying to the travel agent, "I want to go where troubles 'melt like lemon drops,' way above the chimney tops." O lady, may I go with you if you find the place? It has been so long since I laughed. Putting some color on my cheeks today, I had to smile a bit to get it symmetrical. I looked so phoney smiling with my lips when my eyes were empty and listless. Looking in the mirror, I discovered I had aged ten years in just a month's time—the rings under my eyes, the lack of expression in my face and eyes, and the gauntness in the contours of my face. They say women don't get older, they get better—better than what? Another cliche. . . .

July 18: People have been asking Bill, "What is the matter with Barbara?" They assume I am sick because I seldom go out now, and they keep telling him I should really see a doctor. They mean a head doctor, I am sure. If they only knew—wow! I'm sure it is much easier to pray for people from afar than to invest some time and love in their healing process.

If I survive this, you better believe that I will know more how to love and care for others who are hurting. After knowing the heartache of this child going into homosexuality, I have gradually been accepting the blanket of God's comfort. Maybe from this stinging experience I can help lighten the pain for others, if I don't die before I get through this. They say the only difference between a rut and a grave is three feet. Or is it that a rut is a grave with the ends knocked out?

July 23: Had a good session with Dr. Wells today. He says a child cannot evaluate a friend as long as he is defending him. Sexuality has become inverted in both Larry and his friend. Larry had identified with me and now he resents that. Guilt will erode the personality fast. Larry is bursting out in anger. He will seek help when the relationship is ended. He is afraid of me and his deep feelings have not yet surfaced. The chink in his armor is obvious—letting his friend take such advantage of him. Larry was playing the parent role with him. Pressure brings out these defects in people who mutually need each other.

If Larry should call (a miracle in itself) I am to talk with him on an adult level. A love object makes people rationalize anything and Larry has used his friend as his love object. Deceit is hurting him now. I cannot accuse, or assume. Larry's guilt is heavy.

Where is he spiritually? Knowing all this about erosion of personality and change is worthless and wasted unless Larry surfaces sometime soon.

Do you know the height of wasted energy? Telling a hair-raising story to a bald-headed man. Now I am telling jokes to myself to keep my sanity. Only I am not laughing at them.

I have not been able to think outside my own cloudy mind about how Bill and Barney are getting along. When I move around the house I am like a zombie, doing only absolutely necessary things. A really full day for me is to bring in the morning paper, read the obits, throw it in the trash, open some dog food, lie down until supper, and then call Bill to bring home a barrel of chicken, while I just stay in bed and continue this semi-invalid life. I think I am going through an identity crisis and an energy crisis at the same time. I don't know who I am and I am too tired to find out.

I do get dressed on the days when I have to see Dr. Wells, so the neighbors know I am alive anyway—but not well. If I go to the market to get some necessary groceries, I come home with things we don't need. I buy the kind of orange juice Larry likes; his special soap; Pepsi, which he drinks; and I cannot get my heart to admit that he is not here.

No one will drink the juice or the Pepsi because he is gone. We used to sing the chorus, "Gone, gone, gone, gone, yes, my sins are gone." I could sing, "Yes, my sons are gone!" But I do have one dear son left. Barney is quiet and pensive—probably worried about me because I have been acting so weird and crying so much for a month. Whenever I am up to the bathroom or in the kitchen, he is working away in the garage or talking to his friends as they work on motorcycles. I do want to talk in depth to him, but I have to get my own emotional life under wraps before I can talk much about this. Lord, take care of Barney and Bill while I am so "out of it" right now. They don't know what to do to help me, and I sure can't tell them.

July 24: Somewhere back in my mind something is percolating. Some funny ideas are coming out from down deep inside. How long will it be before my face reacts to some humor? I got up enough energy today to write to some top evangelical leaders who are supposed to know the answers. I am expecting any day now to open a letter with a magic formula from these spiritual giants to erase all this dilemma—some magic solution to help. . . .

July 25: I just stayed in bed all day and counted the roses on the wallpaper in my bedroom. The air-conditioning vents have 240 holes in them, counting the ceiling. There are 500 roses in the wallpaper pattern on the side wall. It was not a real enriching day for me. I'm entitled to a free day.

July 28: Seven years ago today Steve was killed. I let my mind dwell on that day and the subsequent events. I realized we cannot dwell on the past but have to move on—to what? I preferred the past events to what I had to face now. Is there another mother who is going through these mental gymnastics as I am? Trying to peel herself off the wall or ceiling? To be with her would be nice!

Anxiously I've been waiting for answers from my spiritual authorities, waiting for them to explain how a Christian can get into homosexuality. A couple of amazing responses came today!

One authority told me the Antichrist would be homosexual because the Bible says he will have no desire for women! Why hadn't I heard that in my years of training in a Christian college? Probably because we never mentioned homosexuality, and being gay meant being happy in those days. Now this information from him was certainly not going to rate him too high on my totem pole. Can you imagine writing this to a mother with a bleeding heart?

Who cares? I don't care at this point if the Antichrist is homosexual, bow-legged or cross-eyed! That letter registered a zero with the rim rubbed out!

Another letter said that Larry's habits, conversation and reactions are as they are because he has been exposed. He will be bounced back from the devil and good will come from this. I'm thinking to myself, Sure, after all, it's not *his* kid. I can bounce back from the moon for all the help that letter is!

Another letter says homosexuality is a demon spirit and we should take Larry immediately to a place in Florida where they can fast and pray for him, and then submit him to deliverance sessions where the demon of homosexuality will be cast out of him. The letter also suggested I mail an article of Larry's personal clothing first; this would be prayed over with the specific request for the unclean spirit to leave him. Scripture verses about defiling the body and a reprobate mind were included—all of which totaled up to another fat zero for me.

Well, Lord, it is back to just you and me again— and my "Joy Box." I have several things in it now besides my original poems. I have some little two-inch dolls with funny faces on them which make me smile. I am still down in the dark well, but God has promised not to forsake me. How good it would be, though, to have someone to cry with sometime.

Bill insists this is just a phase. He has not accepted that we have a real honest-to-goodness problem. He prefers to think it will pass—like the summer. Dr. Wells says it is too late in Larry's life for it to be a phase. Larry's behavior is typical of one who wants to keep it covered at all costs. He says Larry has to face the consequences of reality. So far, the entire deal has cost him nothing. He will not seek help until he is wounded, preferably by his lover. Larry hates me now, Dr. Wells says, because my finding out has probably prevented him from keeping on with the relationship with his lover. The outcome is not encouraging. We must be realistic and can accept it better when we have all the black facts in front of us. It is black—jet-black.

9

Survival Notes: Three

July 29, 1975: I must learn to focus on the problem-solver, who is Jesus Christ, and not on the problem. No one realizes I know that; but the problem is so big and looms so huge that all I can think about is homosexuality.

Dr. Wells also says I am childlike. I am glad he didn't say childish. But because I am so childlike I have not accepted the depths of this. Who wants to? He keeps saying that my childlike qualities are so entwined with Larry that I am suffering more. More than what? More than Larry? Dr. Wells says it is the mothers who disintegrate in these situations. I found out where all the flowers went in the song—they turned into blooming idiots. I still haven't found any *mothers* who are survivors in this kind of situation.

I am determined, no matter how much I hurt, that nothing is going to make me give up on finding a way out of this painful pressure. God is with me. God is in me and I am in Him. But I hurt so much from Larry's absence, not knowing where he is, and being unable to include him in family fun again.

Coming home from Dr. Wells' office today, I saw a red VW like Larry's on the freeway. A blond-haired boy was driving it, and a little Jesus sticker was on the back. Instinctively I pressed on the accelerator. My heart was pounding—how thrilling if it were Larry and I could see he was all right! My heart sank as I leveled with the VW and discovered it was not Larry, after all. Would I go through life looking for blond-haired boys driving red VW's? Would I never be free from the continual search for him on the freeway, in the supermarket? It seems logical that I might see him someplace—he has to be around. But Los Angeles is a big metropolis. Someday I might see him—could be tomorrow.

July 30: I actually passed a mirror in the May Company and didn't see that pained expression on my face. Maybe these counseling sessions are helping erase the strain on my countenance. Actually I looked almost calm. Perhaps I have now moved off the panic button and am beginning to vibrate less. It is the nature of healing to have a beginning, a middle and an end. I must remember at the beginning that there is an end. I will be healed in time. It's hard to accept the fact that everything takes time in this age of fast foods and instantly replaceable everything. But healing is like a lightning bolt—full of ups and downs, dramatic leaps and then depressing backslides. If I know this, I can understand the healing process is underway.

August 1: Today is the beginning of a beautiful new month. I love a new month, tearing off the old calendar. I changed the sheets, shaved my legs, took a long luxurious bath, and am planning on going out for dinner with Bill tonight. Today I am really going to pamper myself.

If I had a physical injury I would get flowers, fruit and a backrub; but I have an emotional injury, and people expect me to perform as usual. The world does not accept the fact that emotional pain incapacitates. I will spend the day doing some things I really enjoy—having a double dip ice cream cone with sprinkles on it at noon, and ending it with warm milk and cookies when I go to bed. I think for this one day I can deposit

Larry in God's hands. First Peter 5:7 tells me I can cast my cares on Him, and Larry is a care. So I am giving him to God for all day today. It is O.K. for me to need comforting. It's O.K. for me to be taken care of for a while. I know the emotional wound is real, disabling and painful, but I can enjoy the rose garden even if it has thorns. Just for today I am going to isolate myself from Larry—I'm determined to wrap myself in my own little "blankie" and have a good first of the month for August. If I can do this for just *one* day, that will be a big step out of this black pit I have been in for so long. I should say a step up, not out. That will take a longer time, to get *out* of it.

August 4: Dr. Wells says that unless God performs a miracle I have to prepare for the possibility of never seeing Larry again. I am to make no offers to help him even if he comes asking for help. I know I will have to keep on seeing Dr. Wells to reinforce this idea because I would melt at the first phone call from Larry, asking for anything, at this point. Dr. Wells repeats over and over that Larry must first suffer, to be so hurt that he will seek help on his own. He has to *want* help. This sounds so ironic—to make your kid suffer so you can help him.

I must consider the high rate of suicides among homosexuals, Dr. Wells says, and when I have actually faced this in reality, then I will have accepted the situation. But I do believe in miracles—I do believe God hears our prayers. I do believe this is the Lord's battle, not mine. Hasn't He brought me from the deep black pit of depression to where I am now? At least I can see I have progressed some in recent weeks; reading through my diary, progress is obvious. I surely am not out of the pit, but at least I am not where I was. When you reach the end of your rope like I did in June, you have to tie a knot in the rope and climb up—and tying the knot was a bit of a miracle even for me. I have inched my way painfully up that rope back to reality, and some healing is taking place,

I am listening to tapes avidly now, particularly from Dr. Walter Martin's Bible class at Melodyland, and they have given me so much direction. I used to detest tapes and "canned" messages; but now when I walk around the house, instead of looking like a zombie, I am more like a zombie carrying a tape machine.

Someone sent me a couple dozen tapes by various speakers. Listening to a tape somehow drowns out the thought of homosexuality for the time being. My mind is allowed to focus on something else. The consuming thoughts of the homosexual lifestyle seem to be lessening as I listen to messages based on God's Word and practical psychology. How many hang-ups we Christians have on so many subjects! Some of us are so narrow-minded we would only have to use one earring! How self-righteous we are.

September 15: For the past couple weeks I have just buried myself in tapes and found they have been a real source of diversion and growth. Dr. Martin has fed me tapes over and over, and I am beginning to see an acceleration of healing in my thinking process. His strong presentation has given me light in the dark way. I have been up doing my housework lately, preparing meals, and carrying the tape recorder around with me like a precious companion. My eyes have some expression again; I am beginning to come out of an emotional prison.

I am beginning to see results—and a couple have been sort of unusual! I had the tape player in the bathroom one day, and some neighborhood kids were out swimming in the pool. A little girl answered the phone out on the patio. It was for me. I heard her say, "Yes, Mrs. Johnson is home, but she is in the bathroom and there's a man in there with her." I nearly died, wondering who was on the other end of the line; and then realized that whoever it was probably died also— hopefully from laughing. So wherever I've gone, I've had Dr. Martin with me, along with Dr. David Seamonds, Dr. James Dobson, and occasionally for some balance songs by John Hall and Roger McDuff.

I've learned that a renewing of the mind can come only from one direction—*above*. Larry needs a renewing of his mind. Some of the tapes I have heard are about cleansing of the heart, washing out all the nagging doubts and fears. God can transform a life from domination to freedom. He can give us new desires. We need to bring our feelings under God's control by bringing them to the Cross. God can recreate Larry and release him from this bondage.

I received a letter from a girl who had been into homosexuality and what she wrote helped so much:

> I no longer want to be known as an ex-homosexual—not because of the stigma attached to it, but because that is such a limiting and inaccurate description of me. I'm so much more, so very much more. I am a woman; I am a natural brunette, I am a child of God. Because I am a growing Christian there are many things in my past which are no longer part of my life. But I don't call myself an ex-TV addict, an ex-smoker or an ex-chocolate fiend! Yet I was hooked on all of those things as long as I was hooked on homosexuality, and they were no less sinful. Well, just as I no longer want to find my identity in being an ex-homosexual, I want to help people other than homosexuals and have fellowship in depth with people other than ex-homosexuals.

This young woman's testimony was saying what I had wanted to hear but which others were not saying. Literature on coping with homosexuality was still scarce and some of the letters which had come to me were so confusing. They actually caused me to regress rather than make progress in finding out how to help myself or Larry through this maze of misinformation.

September 21: I had a beautiful letter from a local pastor today whom I had written to with questions on homosexuality. He said, "God has not negated Larry because of his sin. . . . Think of him as a lost sheep, and learn the causes and cures for this emotional disturbance. Thinking of him as someone who is ill will free you to pray for the healing power of the Holy Spirit to invade and liberate him." What healing balm was in those words for me! Somehow my anger and trauma is being slowly replaced by love and compassion for Larry. I have stopped feeling as if I'm suffocating. Thinking of Larry as a lost sheep, being isolated and alone, is a new concept.

How many times in his life Larry must have been hurt, as he is sensitive in nature. How easy it is to love him or would be if I knew how to reach him. I would tell him that I love him even more now because I can see how he must have struggled with this sexual-identity problem. Wherever he is, I want him to know my love has never stopped. It's pretty hard to let it flow, though, when you haven't seen someone you love in months.

October 1: How neat—another new month. Dr. Wells told me that I am in the healing stage now. I don't know exactly when I left the panic stage and moved into surviving, but it is nice to have a professional person admit to some progress. This is another new month to anticipate some good thing. This could be the month we hear from Larry. Dr. Wells helps me get some balance in this adjustment period, but I am seeing him less now since I have been finding comfort through listening to the tapes.

I have accepted the seriousness of the situation. I know the suicide rates are high among homosexuals. I know that if Larry could survive this long without contacting us, it is entirely possible he will never come home again. His new lifestyle is more important to him than his relationship to his family.

It is raining today. I think I'll make chili for supper and enjoy the rain on the tin roof of the back porch. I wonder if Larry misses having chili on a rainy night and the fun times here with so many young people around? Maybe he is celebrating the new month in a way I don't understand.

Someone sent me a card today which says, "Dear God, I have sinned against heaven and against You. I am no longer worthy to be called Your child. My child, I know, I know. . . . *But my Son is forever worthy to be called your Savior."* People say sometimes we deserve this or that. I am thankful we don't all get what we deserve, or none of us would make it to heaven. I will keep that card for my "Joy Box," which is accumulating more and more now. When I look through this special box, I find my spirits lifting as I recall some verses which have helped me, and some notes I have collected over these past months.

October 15: The Los Angeles *Times* states that the choral group Larry sings with is performing at the Music Center in two weeks. That is so exciting! I am sure he'll still be singing with them. I called my sister, Janet; she will be flying out to spend a week with me. We can go together to hear Larry sing. What a thrill it will be to see him after all these months! I'll rent binoculars, of course, and have the best seats available near the front so we can really see him well.

October 21: The night at the Music Center has come and gone. Janet and I got all decked out in our finest attire. I had a tape recorder in my purse. (Although the rules at the Music Center forbid taping I thought that just in case we talked with Larry it would be so super to get something on tape.) The curtain went up. All the kids were in their colorful costumes amidst a sea of flashing lights; their faces were animated.

Without the aid of the rented binoculars, I quickly located the smiling son we hadn't seen for four months. I never took my eyes off Larry during the entire first half of the show. I drank in his every expression. He looked good, a bit thinner than when he left home. But his eyes looked bright and his color was good.

We were sitting close to the front—a big mistake—for just at the intermission the house lights came on and with the binoculars in my hand I spotted Larry's face when he looked into the audience and saw me. I was so excited when his eyes caught mine and felt for a second that he showed some elation at seeing me. I was even hoping that after the performance we could go backstage and congratulate him. What a shock we were in for! After the intermission the curtain went up and there, in the place where he was supposed to stand and perform, was a void. Larry was gone. He had apparently grabbed his clothes from the dressing room and bolted!

As the group sang "Tie a Yellow Ribbon 'Round the Old Oak Tree" without Larry, I found myself wondering if there would ever be a time when we could tie a yellow ribbon someplace and let Larry know the welcome mat was out for him. All he needed to do was come home, and we would have yellow ribbons all over the place for him. My heart was concrete again—the old football-crushing feeling back in my chest. The rejection dropped on me like a lead balloon. I could feel myself sinking back into where I was that night at Disneyland in June. All the old anxiety had descended on me again. Walking out of the Music Center, my feet felt as if they had bowling balls chained to them again. I must see Dr. Wells tomorrow. Explaining all this to him might help some, but I doubt it.

October 30: It's O.K. to feel anger. Let it out safely. Kick a pillow. Kick a bed! A parked car in a deserted place, like the dump, makes a good "scream chamber." So does playing the piano at full crescendo. If anger is channeled and dissipated in these harmless ways, it will go away and the hurt will heal.

It's O.K. to feel low key for a while. I am stronger now. I have dealt with loss and have grown through it. I can't settle for just surviving and healing. The growth has to continue. Giving is the greatest joy to help healing. There is an ebb and flow of healing and growing. I am having an ebb for now, but it will heal. I am angry at Larry for walking out of the concert, but I am rejoicing that he looked so well. I have mixed emotions (like when your mother-in-law drives over a cliff in your new Cadillac); they are all scrambled up. I am glad I got to see him, even through the binoculars, and he is evidently well and in good health. That is something for which to praise the Lord.

November 20: With the holidays coming up, Dr. Wells says this will be a very difficult time for me. He wants to schedule some extra time—expects me to need it, no doubt. I have survived other holidays with terrific losses, so I guess this will be just another one.

I will concentrate on listening to tapes for the next couple weeks, and just absorb as much as I can. Some people are like blotters: they soak it all in and get it all backwards. I try to soak it in but seem to need to hear the same tapes over and over to understand the message. I've learned to appreciate Dr. Martin so much through his messages. I'd like to ask him how a Christian can be a homosexual. If anyone would give me a straight answer, I know he would.

December 14: Today is my birthday. I didn't expect a card or anything from Larry but Barney wrote me a very precious note. He has become even more special in the past few months since I have been going through this panic. He has a quiet charm that I can't resist.

Barney has had several minor traffic violations and, because he is under eighteen, I have had to go with him to traffic court. We go early in the day and have our breakfast at a restaurant and then spend the morning sitting in the courtroom, while they call roll for all the juveniles with traffic tickets. By the time we get out of there it is time for lunch. So we've been stopping on the way home to have lunch together, and I am getting to spend some *quality* time with Barney!

Sitting in the hot traffic court with nothing to do and no one to talk to except each other, we have had opportunity to talk about many things—some for the first time. It is difficult to talk to him when he is usually in the garage spinning a motorcycle engine. So I even praise the Lord for all the days in traffic court.

December 16: I imagine Larry is having a painful time as the holidays approach. He always enjoyed trimming the tree and decorating the mantel. Spraying all the Brazil nuts gold and mailing packages had been such fun.

Bill has decided it would be easier for me if we just reserved a nice room in Anaheim for the four days around Christmas to get away from the loneliness of the house. This is his attempt to ease things for me. Anaheim is the logical choice since Melodyland Christian Center is where we go to church. Actually, all the horrible memories of last June in Disneyland—which is very nearby—don't make it very inviting for me. But then, I have to get over that.

We have decided on four days at Anaheim to rest, watch TV, and hope that we can survive Christmas without too much nostalgia. Maybe we'll pretend it is just a regular week and not Christmas. But the TV will be geared to Christmas and the music, the bells and all the Christmas festivities will be everywhere.

Last Christmas Larry had written a piece which we wanted to use on our Christmas cards this year. We didn't, in view of his disappearance, but what he wrote is so meaningful and so typical of Larry and his spirit.

Just think, Larry wrote this a year ago, when life was beautiful—all cherries and no pits.

REFLECTIONS LIKE RAIN

Reflections of light on the crowded evening streets meet the winter rain. People pushing, shoving, crying, laughing, revive the Christmas spirit only to have it wither and melt with hurt, grief and sorrow. "You buy me a shirt, I'll buy you a tie" is all the spirit hears. The cries of selfishness ring loud through many homes of holly tinsel and mistletoe. "I want this, and I want that," is said unendingly. As the spirit, the Christmas spirit, the broken spirit, is lost in a world of hatred, war and proud people. But still the real spirit lives on in the hearts of many—those that know Him and know of His love. His love that makes your heart at peace, your life filled with joy. He loved so much He died for us to save us all if we but believe. And still, some still reject His love and live a life of ego. "Is it not His birthday we celebrate?" The spirit poses the question. He gave His life to set us free. This Christmas I gave my life to Him. Now, like the reflections of light on the crowded evening streets that meet the winter rain, my life reflects His love.

Just a year ago Larry had shown so much caring, so much thoughtfulness. Is it possible that this young man, who let this flowing message come from his heart a year ago, is gone from us to a life which is the opposite of love and God?

I read the paragraph over a few times and then tucked it away, thinking that perhaps another Christmas we would put it on a Christmas card as our message to the world. A year ago it thrilled me to read it. Now it only makes the wound in my heart bleed again. Tears flow—hearts bleed—time goes on.

December 24: If I can get through this Christmas, I can get through anything. This evening Barney went to his girlfriend's to open presents, and Bill is at the hotel watching a Christmas program and eating some popcorn he brought along from home. (He likes it better than the kind you can buy.) About 9 P.M. I could no longer stand the TV and the Christmas music. The urge to "break out" was so strong I had to get in the car and just drive someplace—anyplace. I didn't know where the nearest dump was in Anaheim, or I could have gone there. After Tim died, I found I could drive up to the dump and just cry by myself and feel so much relief from the isolation I was feeling.

Our other Christmas Eves had been bright with memories of friends, twinkling lights on the tree, the player piano going with lots of people around singing; and we always had the Christmas story told that night. What a contrast it was for me to drive around in the car, aimlessly, just trying to avoid memories of the past. Would I ever get out of this prison of memories? I drove by Disneyland. Even that had closed early to allow the employees to have the evening with their families. The motels on Harbor Boulevard sparkled with colorful lights and people were carrying packages in and out of the holiday-decorated hotels surrounding the Disneyland area. I came upon an A and W root beer stand and saw someone moving around, so I drove in there. The car hop said they were closing for Christmas Eve, but she was kind enough to get me a root beer.

Everyone is with their families—I have two dear sons and a loving husband—yet here I am sipping an unwanted root beer on Christmas Eve while the music is playing "Silent Night." It is silent all right! It is dead for me.

My self-pity lasted long enough for the girl to tell me they had closed and wanted the mug back. She wished me a "Merry Christmas" and mechanically I said the same to her, with tears ready to burst out of my eyes the minute she turned her head.

Sitting at the A and W, I saw the lonely figure across the street, a young man in Marine clothes, hunched under the weight of a seabag perched on his shoulders. I wondered if there was someone still waiting for him, or if anyone knew he was coming home at all. I remembered the Christmas Eve when Steve brought his buddy from the Marine camp home with him for Christmas, and how warm and bright the house was. Happy memories of other Christmases flooded my mind. My heart cried out to that lonely-looking Marine, for he suddenly was my own son and my own ghost—the soul of us all—driven by this yearly call, "Come Home."

Backing out of the parking area, I thought of Bill eating his popcorn at the hotel, trying by getting engrossed with TV to dismiss the losses we had experienced. Barney was enjoying his girlfriend's family and they were enjoying his company. I was having my own private self-pity party, and only God knew where Larry was.

I know Larry is God's property and He will take care of him ultimately But it hurts so much not to hear from him, not to see him. How could he walk away from a loving family who cares so much for him? If he were dead, how would anyone know who he belonged to? How do they trace people who are suicide victims or found with no identification lying in the street?

Before we left home for our visit in Anaheim, I had wrapped some packages for Larry along with others for the rest of the family. I guess I unrealistically anticipated that he might send someone with a note; or perhaps it was a way of helping me to feel he was still a part of us to buy some things for him. Some were just fun things, and his stocking was filled as usual with some goofy gifts which made us all laugh.

December 27: Christmas Day itself is a blur to me, except that the next day I welcomed the idea of leaving Anaheim and going back home. I didn't want Bill to think I didn't appreciate his loving gesture in taking me away for a few days, but it actually made me homesick, even though we weren't far away.

How relieved I was to get back to our home. I saw the stockings still in place, and the carefully wrapped gifts nestled under the shining tree. I threw myself on the bed and once again those wails escaped from within me, the same uncontrollable sobs that had burst out that day last June.

I guess the manner of crying is determined solely by the personality of the individual suffering the loss, and there is obviously no right or wrong way to express our grief over the pain. Somehow gentle, soft crying didn't express the torn-up feeling I had. I had to allow this to come out of me. To cry is O.K. To cry is helpful. To cry is healing. This was an acute attack of grief which was triggered by Christmas nostalgia; and, as Dr. Wells has pointed out, having regression is normal in the process of grief. I knew it was healthy to express my feelings, to unload my emotions; it was good medicine to help restore wholeness. Dr. Wells had explained to me that letting go in grief would make me integrated and whole. Expressing feelings in the grief process would bring me relief to deal with my loss. That had worked with losses in the past, so certainly this heavy crying now would help me get the pieces together.

How long will it take, I wonder?

December 28: The trigger has gone off during the holidays for me, setting on fire all the emotional embers which had been cooling off. Grief is work, and these bouts with weeping, depression, longing, guilt and anger just have to come out. I've been through six months of this. I thought I was in the healing process. Could the holiday time have caused me to regress this far? I need to see Dr. Wells to achieve some balance in my thinking because I am thinking in circles again. I want to think of Philippians 4:8, but all that races through my mind is Yankee Doodle, feathers, Tinker Bell fairies, and "homosexual."

December 30: I am functioning again in my home. Except for my sister and two close friends, no one knows about Larry. They assume he has been away at college and we've just directed the conversation away from him. I signed his name on a few Christmas cards for relatives and on others we signed the family name, so that eliminated some questions. I've forced myself to perform some tasks because Dr. Wells has explained to me that inactivity could lead to a breakdown. I figure that if I keep moving and keep active, it will be staved off. A cemetery still sounds inviting to me, but not the "Home for the Bewildered" at this point. If I tell people we haven't seen Larry in six months and don't know where he is or what he is doing, that would only lead to more questions and more pain. How would you explain that your fine, upright twenty-year-old son has told you he is a homosexual and then has disappeared into the shadows? I've found it easier to pretend, to keep up a facade or say he is on a trip than to have to face people and explain something we don't understand ourselves.

During all these months my search for knowledge (I have done it discreetly without identifying Larry) has brought me little enlightenment. Some have told me it is a demon, some a spirit of homosexuality. Some said it is sin, others said homosexuals were born this way and nothing could change them. I've received advice to mail his clothes and have them anointed or to have deliverance sessions for him. Christians can't have demons, can they? Was it possible that Larry had been inoculated with small doses of Christianity which kept him from catching the real thing? No, I am certain he had a real experience with Jesus Christ early in his life and there is no doubt in my mind that God has lived in his heart since he was a little fellow.

What do I really know about all this? Being open to every viewpoint, I recently got a book on demon possession; but after struggling through a few chapters of it, I decided that my tormented emotional life could not endure the ideas which were presented in the book (although it was written by a well-known Christian educator). So I must zero in on obtaining more material which will comfort me rather than explain a dimension I don't want to understand anyway.

What is important is that I can survive this! Regardless of where Larry is or what he might be doing, my life has to become whole so that I can be the person God intends me to be. I will bear this unbearable load with God's help. After all, until I can be swimming by myself, how can I help someone else who is drowning?

I have been drowning myself in six months of grief, self-pity, and guilt; now, to take such a nose dive over Christmas holidays is like sliding back in that black pit of depression—and I am not going back down there. No way.

December 31: I have written pages and pages of survival notes. This is the end of the year 1975. This is the last of my survival notes. I have come through the emotional surgery of 1975—without benefit of anesthesia. I feel as if I've been chopped in half, and had my heart cut out. But I have survived! As the year comes to a close today, so do my survival notes. From here on, I have promised God that with His help I am only making *progress* notes because we already know I have survived. Tomorrow is the beginning, a new month. I, who have always loved a new month, have a *new year!* 1976 is going to usher in a year of *progress* for this gal.

I have let anxiety come aboard and keep me awake at night. I have let worry drill holes in my hull and the anchor that tumbled off my boat is dragging and snagging at the bottom. I have wrestled with a past that has been fractured and wounded. When God forgives, He forgets. He is pleased to use any vessel, just as long as it is clean—*today*. It may be cracked or chipped, it may be worn; but the past ended one second ago. As we start this new year, I am clean, filled with His Spirit, and God's glorious grace says: Draw the anchor, trim the sails, look ahead. I have been stuck on that swampy lagoon long enough. It is time to get out into the mainstream where there is fresh water, and into the flow of life where there is action, there is life, there is newness. This new year can be a fresh start. Proverbs 24:16 in the Living Bible reads, "Don't you know that this good man, though you trip him up seven times, will each time rise again?" 1976 will be my year to *rise again*.

10

Progress Notes

How exciting to have a new year! This is a new start—a time for beginning again. God specializes in new beginnings; the cry of the newborn baby reminds us of that. The flowers breaking into bloom with the coming of spring tell us that. And so does the sun rising over Mount Baldy, announcing the arrival of a new day. This year of 1976 is going to be a new beginning for me. God delights in touching broken people and making them whole. This is going to be my year to be restored. God's special adhesive glue is going to cement together the brokenness of my spirit and my heart, and this is my year of beginning again—fresh, clean and new with the Lord.

For the past six months I have searched for answers about Larry and nothing has made sense to me. I know that compassion rather than condemnation is my responsibility toward Larry; and certainly during these months my emotions of anger and rage have turned to compassion and love. I want God's attitude of love toward the sinner (although we know He hates the sin) to be my attitude also.

Looking back, my frantic search for understanding suddenly seems pointless. The truth is as Deuteronomy 29:29 says, "The secret things belong to the Lord"

(NASB). Larry belongs to God. I am going to rest in that knowledge. I have survived thus far and overcome the months of isolation—now let's see how God works in 1976 to make me more of an overcomer. Maybe Larry will let God make him an overcomer too.

Someone wrote me that we are all made of metal—some good, some mediocre. "There is no reason to temper mediocre metal," they said, "because all the tempering in the world won't make it really good. But those whose quality of metal is high had better get ready because they are about to be tempered."

Happy New Year to me! 1975 is over. Throw the old calendar out with its pain and mistakes on each page and start with a new slate. Philippians 4:8 is my verse to repeat daily for the month until I have it translated into my mind and heart. My mind can dwell on what I choose and that will capture me. It is not something I do once and stop, but I must do it hourly, daily, again and again, minute by minute.

I can choose to think on godly things, and the peace of God will be with me. Recently, I gathered my courage and wrote out a question for Dr. Martin to answer on a piece of paper. Before slipping it into the question box, along with the deluge of other questions from class members, I wrote on the front of my folded note: "This one, this one! I need to know an answer from you." And I attached a giant stick of gum to the paper so it wouldn't just be shoved down in the barrel of questions.

Much to my delight, Dr. Martin answered my question with such insight and perception that for me it was like the lifting of the shade on all the dark areas of my mind, and assuring me that what I had learned was right. Larry is God's property. I could give him to God and trust Him to work.

Here is exactly what his answer was, as I transcribed it later from the tape of the class session:

Question: Can a twenty-year-old Christian

young person be hooked into homosexuality?

Absolutely! A Christian can get hooked into sin. Yes, a twenty-year-old Christian can fall into fornication; adultery, yes; drugs, yes. Christians may be tempted and fall into sin even after they become Christians. One can fall into all kinds of evil. The magnificence of Christianity is that Jesus Christ will not let you stay there. He has the power to get you out and keep you out!

He won't let you stay there and I'll tell you why. One, you are His property! You are not your own. You were purchased with a price—the blood of the cross. If you think you are going to become a Christian, fall into some sin, stay in them and *be happy,* then you should think again—because you'll be miserable! And not only that, if you persist in the sin, He might destroy your physical body in order that your spirit be saved. 1 Cor. 5:5: "He will deliver you to Satan for the destruction of your body that your spirit be saved at the day of the Lord Jesus."

Question: Can we hope for his return to God?

If the child belongs to God, either God will bring him to repentance and healing or God will judge. But one thing you can count on, if the child really has been the Lord's, the Lord is going to give special attention to that child! The Lord never gives up on His children. How many people in this room at one time or another have slid back from your faith—that is what the word "apostasy" means. Be honest now, you miserable hypocrites—sitting there with your hands in your laps! Never backslid, eh? I have to raise mine. Now, did the Lord Jesus forgive me? Amen! Did He restore me? Amen! Do I love Him? Serve Him? Witness for Him? Amen!

God always looks for the prodigal. The prodigal is His son. Never forget that! I'm not going to debate whether one can be saved and then lost. God gives only one kind of life. You know what kind that is? Eternal life! I cannot imagine anyone who has had even a little taste of that life rejecting it forever. And if you won't "walk the line" (to paraphrase that great theologian Johnny Cash), that line becomes a *rope* around your neck.

I say this many times to people in very educated circles, and it sounds ignorant but has great truth in it. This is a cosmic law: no one, no way, no how, can get away with nuthin'!

Our young friend may think he can; but somewhere down the line when he is trying hard to forget all about it, God is going to get his attention. The Lord told Israel that it's sudden when it comes upon you and you don't know it. He says, "I will remember you." He is remembering His prodigal son.

God will always have the last word. He tells you what you should do—and then He graciously hounds you until you say, "Yes, Lord!" There are some Christians who die before their time, because the Lord cannot trust them to hold on to their commitment, "Yes, Lord."

Yes, you can *hope* for the Lord to touch that boy. Leave him in the hands of Christ and pray for him. And try to get him to some good counseling with a Christian psychologist.

How nice to have that on tape so I can play it over and over. This was the first solid help I had, the first word that I could hope for Larry's eventual salvation. Here was the *Little White Square* in the black, black picture.

February 7: I haven't seen Dr. Wells now for a few weeks. With the encouragement from Dr. Martin I have felt so much less isolated in all this. Though I have come a long way, it is easy to slip back into the tar pit. The shattered feeling I had that my insides were feathers and wet paper toweling is gone. Much of the physical manifestations of anxiety are over now.

I can brush my teeth without gagging and haven't complained that they itched now for several weeks. Would you believe that the TV is full of talk now about homosexuality? Parents appearing on one program looked shattered and hopeless, as I did several months ago. In the course of the telecast, someone mentioned a book called *The Third Sex?,* so I've ordered it from the Christian bookstore. I must admit, I was reluctant to order it because as yet my Christian sisters are still not opening up about what homosexuality is doing in families. "Keep it under wraps as long as it hasn't happened to you," they figure.

I read of a man called Brother Frank, living in San Rafael, who had been a homosexual for twenty-five years. Now he has a ministry called "Love in Action" which helps people who want to get out of that lifestyle with God's help. I called him and explained my situation and the months of separation, and he graciously offered to come down and talk with me. I was nervous about meeting him; yet I want so much for him to tell me how to handle the broken relationship between Larry and ourselves.

To drive way out on Wilshire in Los Angeles to meet an ex-homosexual at night was scary for me, but the desire to get further help was paramount in my mind.

All my anxiety left when this tall, kindly gentleman in a light suit approached me; and his loving spirit and gentle voice assured me immediately that he would minister to my heart and help with the healing process which had begun some weeks ago.

Frank told me that there is no such thing as quick deliverance from homosexuality. Larry's *attitude* toward this sin could change immediately; but God's grace at work in his life would need time to repair habits and responses. No Band-Aids will work.

It takes time to get well, just as it takes time to become a homosexual. Frank told me also to get acquainted with gay literature and learn of the way homosexuality traps young people—know about it sufficiently so that the shock will leave. When I can overcome the disgust and shame, I can relate to Larry without showing my revulsion to homosexuality and he will more readily accept me.

Until Larry comes out and admits his problem, without any more pretense, he cannot defeat Satan. God can bring good, even from such vileness. Homosexuality is a destructive force, more so because as other sexual sins, Christians are ashamed to talk about them. Frank says the more I understand about homosexuals and their problem, the quicker I will be rid of the trauma. He said Larry's reactions to me were triggered because he was exposed; they represent typical behavior in a homosexual who has been found out.

Frank gave me some interesting cassette tapes which helped open my thinking on all this; helping me see how homosexuals are struggling and hurting. They really suffer when God's plan of sexuality gets out of balance, and the balance is delicate. It is a real struggle to come out of that lifestyle, but God will provide the power.

Frank recommended a book, *Growing Up Straight* by Barbara Wyner, which helped some. Also, a book by William Aaron called *Straight* was enlightening. Before reading these books, I thought one just went up to a homosexual and got him to repeat 1 John 1:9; and then away you go knowing they are clean and the problem is over. I didn't know that it is more than a matter of repair—it is a matter of creation. There has to be a healing process. Inordinate desires can be changed; and Jesus is the one who can change them. The first step for the homosexual is to want to be changed. His *feelings,* his *responses,* will take time to fall in line; but they will when his will is set to follow God.

As I listened to Frank's tape, I felt such compassion for these kids who were caught in Satan's trap of homosexuality. Slowly I was beginning to realize that a flood of love was in my heart for all of them, not only for my own son. I felt love for their families who were hurting as I had been hurting. The seed thought was growing in my heart that God was going to use this time of suffering; that from the ashes beauty would come, from the pain there would be blessing. I had learned that I could survive through the power of God, and that it was He who met my need and brought me through the desert. I began to sense that a ministry would be born for parents who were suffering as I had. It would be an outgrowth of my own personal Gethsemane.

March 1: This is a lovely new month. I enjoyed a special surprise today. It was a letter from a mother who had a son in the gay lifestyle. The son had changed and come away from it. I find her letter to be such a treasure and joy; I'll place it in my "Joy Box" and share it with other mothers who need encouragement. She experienced all the feelings I had and she expresses herself so clearly. I love this lady, although I don't know her personally. Praise the Lord for this letter, which I will read over and over and over. It is the first contact I have had with a real honest-to-goodness mother who has survived this same pain. I felt as close to her as to my own sister, after reading about her personal struggle with her emotions.

Dear Barb:

It is hard to describe to anyone the complete loss and dismay you feel when you go through this. I have had no one to talk to other than my husband. We know of no one who has had to go through this same trial. Oh, I know several gays, but as far as I know their families do not know it.

Sometimes I wonder if the wound will ever heal. You wonder why you were singled out to be subjected to this cruel pain. And it is real pain. Your heart is broken, your plans, hopes and dreams are wrecked. Everything that made your life livable is lost. You are physically and mentally ill. You try to eat, and when you eat you vomit bitter gall. You feel betrayed, so you cry yourself to sleep, and you walk the floor half the night. You

say, "God, let me die. I have nothing to live for."
You cry out, "Dear God, why me?" You write reams
of letters, some pleading, some of hate, and you
tear them all up. What is the use? You are up
against a brick wall: where do you go from here?
You want to commit suicide, you hope for a fatal
illness that will take you away from it all.

It is true, you plan your obituary. Death has no
sting—only living is painful. You experience many
emotions—fear, hate, self-pity, recrimination. It
was your fault, or was it your husband's? Was it
worth it all bringing him into the world? The sac-
rifices you made to provide the best of everything.

Did you show him enough love? Did you show
him too much love or give him too much protec-
tion? Perhaps you have not been a good parent
and God is punishing you. And so you go on and
on in circles until you wonder if you are sane.

I could write pages of the worry and fretting
you go through. I remember my mother saying
when one of my brothers died, "When you lose
your husband it is hard because you have lost your
mate, but when you lose your child, you lose part
of your heart and life because you gave him life."
Only mothers can understand the great loss we
feel.

I also collected and read verses and books of
inspiration and I would like to share this with
you, Barbara:

> "The bravest battle that was ever fought,
>   Shall I tell you where and when?
> On the map of the world you will find it not,
>   It was fought by the mothers of men."

And what a battle we were called upon to fight!
The only thing I could think to do was to ask God
for the help to get me through this. I began to realize that in spite of some of the cruel things my
son would say and do, and the indifference he
would show when we tried to get through to him,
I loved him and saw perhaps he was hurting and

suffering also. When he was a little child I could wash his wound and put on a Band-Aid, but how can you put a Band-Aid on a wounded soul? So I began to pray for him, and eventually I began to accept myself better.

Love is a strong power: continue to love your son.

"Love knows no limit to its endurance.
No end to its trust, no fading of its hope—
It can outlast anything.
Love still stands when all else has fallen."

I tried to continue on the best I knew for my family. It is amazing how many times you can polish, dust and paint the same piece of furniture or wall, whether it needs it or not. People begin to think of you as a very fussy housekeeper, but sometimes you cannot remember if you did a room or not; you just have to keep moving. I took up china painting, ceramics, handwork—anything to keep me occupied.

I continued to work on my job, although at times that too had its hardships. People are cruel and love to tell jokes about the more unfortunate. I heard many stories about "queers" and "fags" and my heart would sink a bit more, but somehow you get strength to go on from day to day from the Lord. Then as the days go by and the years pass, you begin to sense a change in your son's life. At first you wonder, is it just a passing fancy? Is he truly seeking answers or is he just covering up? But again time tells you that Jesus Christ has been at work and you begin to see the sunlight again.

Thank you for listening to me and being my sounding board. I have put things in this letter that have passed through my mind for years, and yet I was unable to say or tell anyone, even my own sisters.

May God bless you,
Mary

(Note: This story has a joy-filled continuation: Mary's son is now in full-time Christian ministry, helping others understand the way out of homosexuality.)

March 17: I decided to drive up to San Rafael today and have another talk with Frank. He really gave me encouragement. The fact that he had been an actively practicing homosexual for twenty-five years and had come out of that life, now giving his time and energy working with others, showed me what a real miracle is. He said he felt that Larry had a warm, loving heart, and that the same traits which caused him to become homosexual could also make him an outstanding believer. Satan can wreck and mutilate this loving spirit and turn this godly love into lust, making useless one of the Lord's servants.

Most homosexuals Frank counsels are frightened, lost sheep. A young person deeply attracted to someone can confuse this love with sexual desire and fall; it isn't long before the love turns to bitterness and a hardened resentful, bitter homosexual is born.

It is hard to see these sometimes grotesque individuals whom Satan has twisted, and think of them as tender, idealistic young men; but they once were, before the hurt and confusion entered their lives. Yet, praise God, this trend is reversible. God can remake a damaged life if that life is given to Him in total submission.

Frank reminded me that we are in enemy territory during the time of our sojourn here (1 Pet. 1:17) and that we should prepare our children for the onslaughts of this world, telling them how it really is.

"As Christians," said Frank, "we sometimes live as we would like to think it is rather than how it *really* is. . . . This is a perverse world, and we must not allow any of our flock to be eaten by the wolves. Young people must be told, until they fully understand, what is out there waiting to devour them. . . . Satan has no interest in most of the world—it is already his and he takes little notice of it. He wants what is *not* his; and that tiny part, the Christian part, he is after. Larry has been hurt. You, his mother, must continue to love him. He is in rebellion, but Jesus will bring him home." Frank's words were like a soothing balm to me. I drank in his encouragement.

March 19: Had a long talk with Frank via the telephone. This was pretty heavy stuff but the notes from our conversation will be more indelible if I put them down on paper to study. So here goes:

Frank says Larry had been on an upward spiral. Then something happened to shatter him, and he started on his downward spiral. He probably began to see hypocrisy at every turn; in others, first, and then in his own family. Had he been thinking straight, he would have known that this was not hypocrisy, but just human beings doing their thing—losing their temper, becoming separated from the Lord, failing, yet still being forgiven and restored by the grace of God. But this downward spiral would not allow Larry to think straight, and he was convinced that everything had gone wrong. Things he normally would overlook suddenly became important examples of the hypocrisy that he now saw. Something had come in and shattered his faith. He now obviously feels he has failed God and won't face up to Him.

"Understand how things are now with your son," Frank said. "With his good looks, no doubt he is the center of attraction. Everything is available to him, the rewards of the world are sweet to him. Nothing you can say or do will cause him to give up the worldly pleasures he is now enjoying. Satan is doing his work slowly, the trap of homosexuality is binding him tighter and tighter.

"Larry is finding security in the homosexual way of life. He has a new cause to fight for. It is a heady world, exciting and sexually fulfilling. No one can deny that the world has enticing things to offer. No mom or dad can compete with the delights Larry is now enjoying. You cannot bring him home, but there is one who can. This is the time your faith is tested by fire. This is the time that we all must depend on Christ because we cannot do it ourselves.

"Larry does not yet know the truth about the gay life. It is a shallow, deceptive life," Frank says. "If he lost the way and became disenchanted with Christianity, you can be sure that he will find the deception of the gay life. Those he will think are his friends will disappear, along with his possessions. Someone will tell him he is the only person in his life and the next night be in bed with someone else. He is in for some real pain. The beauty of homosexuality will be stripped away, and he will see the ugly face of Satan under the mask. It will happen, and he will be driven to despair by the realities of the homosexual life.

"He may have to hit bottom before he returns to the Lord—he may become involved with drugs and alcohol. Sometimes the Lord allows us to wallow in degradation, as the prodigal son, before we realize that there are good things in our Lord's house that we have left behind. Satan will take possession of some areas of Larry's life. He is not sick; he is in sin. Christ can deliver him, and it is important that we make him know we love him."

This is pretty impossible, I'm thinking, since we have no way of knowing where he is—haven't seen him now for eight months. "Keep your love in the open," Frank says, "and Christ will do the rest."

If I lose hope in Jesus now, then I have lost everything. Christ is our only hope. The best one is on our side.

"Obviously Larry had high Christian ideals. Someone like that can have a long way to fall. When someone he has admired or looked up to has revealed feet of clay or tried to seduce him, or shared a homosexual experience with him, the shock is sometimes more than a young person can take. The first urge is to fight back to protect one's self and belief. It is hard to realize that the man is only human and has fallen and should be helped and forgiven. The man has hurt him where it is most important—in his faith; and the reaction is to hurl the charge of 'hypocrite.' As this sort of thing occurs more and more often, the picture begins to build in his mind that all Christians are hypocrites and that he has been duped. His beautiful image of Christianity is smashed by reality: Christians sometimes fall. Someone very idealistic cannot accept this; it 'blows their mind,' as the kids say."

Hearing Frank tell me all this was like removing lots of the webs in my mind. The "why" of all this became less important. Just learning to show unconditional love to these hurting kids seems paramount to me now. By letting God's love flow through me to them, God will do the changing. He can bring the healing.

I like that thought I read on a card recently—called "reversal":

"Lord, for so long I thought Your love demanded that I change.

At last, I am beginning to understand that *Your* love changes *me*."

11

More Progress Notes

March 23: This is a heavy day, it is Larry's twenty-first birthday—ordinarily such a festive occasion. To reach maturity in years and have the glorious freedom of being an adult is something wonderful. I think back to twenty-one years ago, and the beautiful baby son he was—so loved, so wanted, such a bundle of dreams for the future. What is he doing to celebrate his birthday? What is one heavy day once in a while, compared to every day being heavyhearted as they were some months ago?

It has been nine months now since we have seen Larry. Just think, I could have had a baby in the nine months he has been gone! Hardly probable but I do think of how much could have happened in all these months with no sign, no calls, no contact—just one special son who has disappeared into the Los Angeles smog.

April 1: Another new month. April is a good month. It represents hope, promise. It's jump ropes, marbles, baseball and mothers pushing strollers. April is mist on the hilltops, rain on the roof, the smell of fresh-turned earth. It is violets, flaming azaleas, gardeners putting out pansy plants. It's buds on the lilacs, rain on weekends, mud on the kitchen floor. April is the month of great stirring. It is the doorway to May—the most gracious month of all.

May 10: Mother's Day has come and gone. Easter was a difficult time, with such an acute awareness of Larry's absence, but I primed myself to pretend Mother's Day was just another day. Nevertheless, the usual fuss was made over mothers at church—the oldest, the youngest, the one with the most kids, etc. There's just no way to escape the "folderol" of Mother's Day. The mother who was being recognized in each category stood up, and then the entire audience clapped as she received a flower or some token of tribute. After the oldest, the youngest one with the most kids, the one with the newest baby, then all the expectant mothers were asked to stand. I found myself wondering how come they didn't ask for all the mothers who had sons who had disappeared to stand up. I didn't fit into any other category—and surely I should qualify for one. Maybe all the "broken-hearted mothers" would be more appropriate. But this thought didn't last long. I praise the Lord for Barney, who is eighteen now. He sent me a cute card with the following note on it: "Things are going to be getting better, Mom. I just know the worst part is over. . . ." Coming from him, this was a treasure far beyond anything money would buy for me.

May 14: It has been eleven months since Larry left. We have nearly passed the full cycle of holidays—Thanksgiving, Christmas, Easter, Mother's Day, birthdays—and now the next one coming up is Father's Day. Just seeing Father's Day cards on the racks sends me into orbit. We have had no messages from Larry, but have learned from someone that he is living in the Westwood area.

It would be possible to hire someone to trace him down, but who wants someone who doesn't want to be found? Nearly a whole year of separation and isolation—worse than death by far. The healing is coming, but it is slow; it is painful. There are many days when

I slip back into the heaviness, but then, with the help of my "Joy Box," some scriptures, or a phone call from my sister (who has never stopped trying to encourage me through all the months of this trial), I take heart and move on. I am not the slow-moving zombie I was back last summer, when I crept around with glassy eyes and an expressionless face. Now I have my usual clear eyes, and I smile and laugh without effort. But the burden of the previous months has taken a heavy toll on my spirit and my looks. I have been drained of the "bubbly" quality people always associated with me in the past.

May 15: Each Thursday I drive down to the Prayer and Share meeting at Melodyland. I enjoy the music and seeing how God works in lives. As usual, today I welcomed the time to just sit and listen and be by myself in the presence of the Lord.

Driving down, I was aware that this suffering would soon reach the full circle of a year. I was tired of the memories, tired of the churning over Larry—tired of giving him to God, and then carrying the heaviness myself. I said out loud to the Lord, "God, I have had enough of this! Whether he kills himself, or if I never see him again, or if you take Larry's life, as you might do, or *whatever happens—he is yours.* I cannot go on one more day with this overwhelming concern for him which has been consuming me for eleven months. The word is 'whatever,' Lord—you do whatever you want with Larry; and whatever you want to do with my life, what is left of it, you can do that too."

I kept repeating to myself that this is the day, this is the day . . . this is the day the Lord has made for me to be *released* from this year of suffering.

Of course I had given Larry to God in the past, and over and over I thought I had taken my hands off and surrendered him to the Lord. But I had been picking up my burden again and bringing it back home to carry around. Like the little poem that says:

As children bring their broken toys, with tears for
  us to mend,
I brought my broken dreams to God, because He
  was my friend.
But then, instead of leaving Him in peace to work
  along with ways
That were my own, at last I snatched them back
  and cried,
"How can you be so slow?"
"My child," He said, "What could I do?
You never did let go!"

The burden was at the Cross. This time it would
stay there.

I went into church and felt a real lifting of my
spirit. The music was comforting; the singing always
lifts me. Then as the pastor called for prayer for various situations, he said, "There is a mother here with
a broken heart." I had heard him say that for eleven
months, and each time I knew it was me. In fact, I had
gone forward a couple times and asked for healing.
Nothing dramatic had happened, although as I look
back, I can see a gradual healing process through
which God brought me so that I might comfort others
suffering the same pain. The pastor repeated his concern for the mother whose heart was breaking, and
suddenly I knew it was *not me*. I wanted to get up and
shout at the top of my voice, "Pastor, it's not me! It's
not me!" For the first time in eleven months when he
talked about a broken-hearted mother, it was someone
else. Always before, I had felt such a drawing or mag-
netic force reminding me that I was the one who was
hurting. Now, finally, I wanted to look around and see
who the poor mother was who had the hurt—because
it was not me!

I practically flew home! My heart sang; the music
just flowed out of me. The only explanation for my
lightness in spirit was that I had allowed God to keep
the burden of Larry. I thought I had given Larry to
God, over and over, but it was not until today when I

really "nailed the burden down" that I felt this surge of relief from all the heaviness in my heart.

When I had finally stopped asking God, "Why me, Lord?" and turned it around to "Whatever, Lord," then the burden actually lifted and I was free in my own spirit to expect God to work.

I can see now that all the hammering on me had made me a better tool. All the pain in the past eleven months would make me strong to help other hurting people whom God would bring into my life. I have survived with only God so far, no real supportive friends; and He has brought me through the isolation, the desperate time, the unreality, and shock of despair. He cares about me. He has not left me alone. He is shaping me, sanding me, pounding on me like precious metal and putting me in the fire. He will not let me burn up. Wasn't it Job who said "Though he slay me, yet will I trust in Him"? and I think when I finally said, "Whatever, Lord," then God knew my hammering was finished. During the drive home, I sang along with John Hall "It's done, yes, it's done," and felt the assurance that God was doing a work. After eleven months of such heaviness, I appreciate the free feeling in my heart. My gift of humor is surfacing now, and I can feel laughter bubbling up inside me.

Yes, the deep gift of joy inside me has been released, and I seem to be bursting with pent-up joy. It's like having my own private fireworks display—an explosion following all the months there had been a tight cap on my humor.

Thank you, Lord, for restoring to me my sense of humor. I had never lost it, really; it was just buried down there, under so much depression that it couldn't get out. Nailing my burden to that cross has made room for this joy to spurt up through my spirit.

May 17: Today started out like any typical busy Saturday. The gardener was pruning the camellias, the pool man was there cleaning the pool, and my heart was still really singing from the lifting of the burden two days ago at Melodyland.

When the phone rang, I expected it to be my friend who was going with me to visit a new mall which is just opening this week. Instead, I heard a familiar voice, one which I had missed for eleven months, saying, "I'm at In-n-Out Hamburgs, and I'd like to bring you a hamburg. What would you like on it?" This voice from the past had its usual cheeriness, the usual boyish sound—and yet sort of hesitant.

For a fraction of a second, I thought of all the things I wanted to do which would be the right things! I didn't want to cry or sound too emotional. I wanted to let Larry know that I was glad to hear from him, and yet not sound too glad so that he would be afraid of an emotional scene if he came home. But of course there was so much excitement and emotion welling up within me that I found it hard to muster a normal-sounding voice to just say, "Oh, anything you get is fine." Larry used to work at that particular hamburger place and knew from experience what I wanted on my hamburgers; but calling was, I think, his way of determining my attitude toward him after so many months of silence.

Hanging up the phone, I sat as though paralyzed for a minute. It would take him about twenty minutes to get home, and in that time I had to run through the house and get all the gay literature and books I had been studying and collecting out of sight.

I didn't want him to be turned off by the fact that I was so obviously making a real study of this subject. I dashed through each room and threw everything that even looked like it hinted of homosexuality under the bed! (I was hiding gay literature from *him?*)

Then I called Frank with the desperate question: "What shall I do? *Larry is coming to see me!*" How can I act sort of aloof when inside I want to hold him like I'll never let go? How can I treat him as an adult and not show any motherly concern? Is there a special button you push that suddenly changes a long-time mother into just a friend to her child? Frank's calm advice helped me to gather my wits together.

Larry's picture was still up on the piano where it had been since he left. I had turned it around for several months because I couldn't bear to look at it and wonder where he was. But it was dusted off, and I knew that when he came in the door and saw his picture in its usual place on the piano, it would signal to him that he was still our son—still loved, still accepted, still part of the family.

After surveying the house and seeing that all was in order for his arrival, I had this sudden, wild impulse to find a baby doll, wrap it all up in a blanket, and then when he came in and asked what's new, I could say, "Well, you have a two-month-old baby sister." After all, he had been gone almost a year and anything could have happened! (It was a far-out idea—but then for him to be coming home was pretty far out too!)

Just then the moment came. I heard Larry struggling with the front door; then he walked in, spilling fries all over the entryway in his efforts to balance the hamburgers, fries and Cokes. I merely said lighthearted things like, "What do you do for an encore, Larry?" (after he had succeeded in spilling the remainder of the fries on the carpet). I was praying desperately that I would not appear too emotional or cry. I was actually thankful for this little *faux pas* of his, so we could concentrate on talking about wet, soggy hamburgers and picking up french fries from the white brick entryway. Small talk can be such a blessing when you are exploding inside.

We collected what was left of the "lunch" and spread it out on the kitchen table. Just Larry and me for the first time in eleven months. I hugged him and told him how good he looked and how glad I was to see him. The dog sniffed him and wagged his tail but wasn't sure who he was, either, at this point. Sitting there, talking of mundane things such as how much the flowers had grown, and how the dog was doing, and how much easier it was to care for the new tile on the kitchen floor was somewhat difficult for me. I had so many questions, but I let him carry the ball in the conversation. He seemed eager to talk—not about anything special, just sort of catching up on what we had been doing. I followed Frank's advice and didn't pump him for any information, and the atmosphere was not as tense as I had been prepared for. Actually, it was as if Larry had been on a long, long trip (to the moon, maybe) and had come home, showing a great interest in what had happened at the house while he was gone. He stayed about an hour and played the piano a bit. It was so good to hear him play some old favorites of his. He loves Bach and the classics, and is exceptionally good at the piano. The pins and needles I had experienced before he came sort of disappeared. It was as if all the separation and pain was like the anguish of childbirth—forgotten when it is behind you.

Perhaps the lifting of my spirit two days ago had been God's special way of wrapping me in His love so that I could show that love to Larry without any traces of resentment or the questions which normally would have spilled out.

I hugged Larry and told him how much we loved him. There was no mention of homosexuality or his lifestyle or where he was living or what he was doing. I knew that any probing would have to be gentle, and it would be difficult to come across with a gentle probe when I wanted so much more information. So I just asked the Lord for an opportunity to use the patience I had learned in the past year. (Patience is the ability to idle your motor when you feel like stripping your gears. And, believe me, I had learned to idle the motor by this time!) Larry didn't seem in a hurry to leave; he took a run through the rest of the house and checked over his room. You would have thought he was from the building and code department by the way he so carefully inspected everything.

Then, being as light as possible, we had some cola and sat in the living room and talked about some neighborhood changes, about the fact that my car had been painted, about the tree in front having been removed because the roots were entwined in the water lines—at least we were *talking!* We were communicating not on the subject I wanted to talk about—but this was *his day.* Since I knew my probes would be too deep and the surgery or wounds were still visible, I would just let him overflow with his thoughts and keep mine tightly zipped up until I had sorted out my feelings myself.

When Larry left, we hugged each other and I said I loved him. His face showed some real expression of appreciation that he had made this initial contact with me. He said he'd come back and see his dad and brother soon. He had borrowed a car to come over, and when he left I stood on the porch and waved him off (which is our usual custom). I waited a minute, as the little car headed down the street, and then I was thrilled to hear the familiar three short blasts from the horn—a special little family signal meaning "I love you."

So funny, that three short honks would send me into such ecstasy! The relief of seeing him, knowing he was O.K., and knowing that he honked that horn three times meant to me that he had made a big step in the healing for which our family had been praying for almost a year.

I sat alone and cried for a while; but they were tears of relief and of joy. When words fail, tears flow. And words surely failed me in those moments. Nothing I did to restrain the flow helped. It was as if all the bound-up feelings and buried restraints were being released at the same time. My emotional "hose" was getting flushed out and a real catharsis was taking place.

According to Psalm 56:8, God puts our tears in His

bottle and enters them into the record He keeps of our lives. I had read that verse in the past and now I am reflecting on how many buckets of tears I must have cried since our devastating night at Disneyland.

May 18: Celebration! How beautiful that God, in love, throws a veil across our way so we cannot see the future. I am able now to thank God for that veil which keeps our future sealed with Christ. We don't know what the future holds, but we do know the one who holds our future.

I have read many good books on grief and sorrow so that I could have something to identify with and help me understand my feelings; and a poem which keeps returning to my mind that I rejoice in now is this:

There is no oil without squeezing the olives,
No wine without pressing the grapes,
No fragrance without crushing the flowers, and
No real joy without sorrow.

I can delight in the fact that I have had a son restored to me again. Yesterday's encounter was not completely like the homecoming of the prodigal because he is still hanging on to his sin; and there are still a lot of barriers in our communication. But it is not a silent brick wall now. It's more like a ventilated screen: we can see and talk to each other, but real heart-to-heart talking is not possible right now. I am just thankful that he came home. I am thankful for a cold, wet, crumbly hamburger shared with a long-lost son who looked so healthy; and for Proverbs 25:25, which says, "As cold waters to a thirsty soul, so is good news from a far country." Larry IS good news to me. Los Angeles, where he has been living, is certainly a "far country"!

How thankful I am for the way my parents built the Scriptures into me in my youth so that they sustained and refreshed me all during these months of desolation.

I've tried to sort things out which might give me clues to help some other parents who might be going through the emotional tug-of-war we have survived. In the beginning, we said we loved him and God loved him, but that he desperately needed help, and that sent him into a real panic.

What about parents who kick their kids out and tell them never to darken the door again? Would they ever come home, even after a long separation, and forgive the parents' responses or reactions?

If we handled the discovery of Larry's homosexual lifestyle "unusually well" (according to most clinicians), and our son disappeared for eleven months— heaven help those who take the opposite approach! I know this is a new beginning for us. We are being groomed for a ministry which will provide the love and caring comfort needed for other parents who are "on the ceiling" as I was when this first happened.

The joy God has given me has to be used for a healing ministry to others who are where I have been and who come for help. I have survived this, and have been an overcomer. The tools of suffering used by God have produced something for His glory. But what is my task? To be a "wound healer"? Could I use this gift of joy I have received in a ministry with others? "Peeling parents off the ceiling" is what I would technically call the ministry, but healing wounds is the primary purpose. There must be many hurting people—parents devastated as I was. Maybe what people mean when they speak of ministering "in Christ" is to be the "interface" between people in conflict—smoothing balm on the brokenhearted. "Wound healer" is not a really joyous label. But it does fit the ministry which is being shaped inside my heart. I feel that my soft, pliable heart is *beating* now, not *bleeding!* What a change from before! Wound healer—binding up the brokenhearted. God could use me for that now! "To bind up the brokenhearted" (Isa. 61:1).

12

Moving from the Panic Button to a Holding Pattern—Without Getting Lost on the Trip!

The next few chapters will be addressed specifically to parents who find themselves in the same situation that we did with a homosexual child. Many principles will apply to other problems, though, so the rest of you may listen in!

There are so many levels of need when it comes to helping people in crises. This chapter is for *you*, so that you can help yourself out of your panic vibration to other awareness besides cyclical thoughts of homosexuality; to where you can start walking down the street without questioning the sexuality of everyone you pass.

Panic is a state of fear in which a person sees only one way out. She will not listen to others; her mind is caught in a fantasized, dreadful future event; and her behavior often appears nonrational. This shock or dazed condition, symptomatic of one's panic level, will give that zombie-appearance as she performs household tasks.

If you find yourself in this stage, you might have difficulty making decisions, even small ones, and your mind may lapse for minutes or hours. It is at this time that you must find some friend in whom you can confide. Just this caring presence will help you to slow down, avoid rash decisions and help you seek competent professional help if you need it.

Of all the mothers who have come to me after learning of their child's involvement with homosexuality, the ones who have come through with the least amount of "scar tissue" are those who have had a listening friend to help reduce the level of anxiety. Mothers in panic most likely will consider suicide and are unreasonable in their responses to most areas of their daily lives. A loving, understanding friend who will allow her to talk and drain off some of the emotion can be a special gift from God at this point. Friends who come across as cold, unfeeling, will not help right now.

A warm, responsive friend—one who has patience and will listen—is essential because talking is therapy. Talking will help sift all those emotions down into some sensible action.

Please don't sacrifice the permanent on the altar of the immediate—a foolish, hasty action such as telling him to get out of your sight and leave the house might give emotional release but will probably jeopardize the relationship with the child forever.

Many parents in their state of fury and emotional upheaval are not controlling their actions. Those wild threats and accusations are not easily erased. To prevent impulsive words and actions you might want to put these words on a placard and tack them up where you see them daily: "I do not want to sacrifice the permanent on the altar of the immediate!"

Matthew 12:34 says, "Out of the abundance of the heart, the mouth speaketh." Your heart is so full of fear, anger, hurt, and a kaleidoscope of feelings that must get off your chest. By unloading yourself of these inner pressures you are unplugging that panic button, and by getting rid of these pent-up emotions you will slowly begin to experience an emotional catharsis. This serves somewhat like an air valve on an inner tube; talking will permit the pressure to escape, and with it will come release.

In one of my sessions with Dr. Wells, soon after Larry's initial acknowledgment that he was a homosexual, I apologized for my continual talking and the spilling out of my feelings, over and over. I told you Dr. Wells' answer earlier, that as long as I was talking I was in less danger of becoming very disturbed, possibly even requiring hospitalization. He explained to me that tensions which are sealed up on the inside can poison us and create even greater pressure. So I continued to see him in therapy sessions and talked on and on. I called my sister, Janet, and often released my feelings in conversations with her. That was of tremendous value to me because she is understanding and feels right along with me; she let me talk and talk. This was a vital part of my therapy, by talking I was unloading my panic. This helped me to live a semi-normal life and not retreat permanently to my comfortable bed with the quilt pulled over my head, withdrawing forever from the weird world of reality.

Language is the "dress" of thought. Every time we speak, our minds are on parade. Now, mothers who are in a state of panic with the accompanying emotional upheaval are not going to make carefully thought-out remarks, or attempt to be profound. (There are two kinds of cleverness, and both are priceless—one is thinking of a bright remark in time to say it; the other, thinking of it in time not to say it.)

One mother confided to me that her homosexual daughter had told her that her "lover" had just lost her own mother in death. The mother retorted, acidly, "Did she commit suicide because she learned her daughter was a lesbian?" This is an example of the type of remark we have to keep in check, though it is probably typical of the way mothers feel. Strong emotions keep coming out in biting words for many weeks after panic is born—but the point is that they should not be said to the child.

Deep-rooted problems require structured counseling by a trained therapist over a period of time, but the type of counseling I am suggesting right now is the "pressure-releaser" type which can be obtained by having a confidante you can trust.

Our Heavenly Father wants us to share our burdens and problems with Him. Talking to God about our problems gives us the opportunity to appropriate His peace. But God's plan is more than vertical. To really know God, we must understand Him in every dimension. On the horizontal level, His perfect plan is for us to "bear one another's burdens" (Gal. 6:2). It is His plan that we extend a helping hand, lend a listening ear, as well as share ourselves and our burdens. Yet, when it comes to homosexuality, Christians are so afraid of jeopardizing their image, or that of their family, that confiding in *anyone* is perhaps the most difficult step in unloading their grief. To admit we have a homosexual child or husband is *extremely* difficult— more so than opening your car trunk *knowing* you'll find a dead body!

In this fear for our image, we are failing to reveal our real need. We stagger beneath the crushing weight of emotional pressure and become emotional phonies, limping along, pretending everything is all right. I know, because I did this for several months.

The hurt is so deep when you learn your child is a homosexual that fear of others finding out grips you like icy fingers, making it almost impossible to reveal your hurt to anyone. Even if you did tell someone, their advice would be meaningless unless they had been through the same experience; and those who have been through it are often silent, stoical, and internalized in their own grief. How, then, can you find someone with a listening ear who can help you siphon off some bad emotions?

Many people have so many hang-ups of their own that they are useless to serve as a sounding board for others. Not everyone has the ability to listen. Most people prefer to give advice or talk about themselves. Finding a suitable confidante, one with whom you can share your feelings and needs, is extremely important. Oh, the inexpressible relief of being able to pour out your thoughts to a friend, knowing they will separate the chaff from the wheat and with a breath of kindness blow the rest away!

When you are looking for a listening ear, one requirement stands out above all others: seek the counsel of the godly, not the godless (Ps. 1:1).

My own conviction is that a good counselor is one who has been *through* problems and has been victorious. You want someone who is a winner! Finding winners is difficult—they are scarce. The "Home for the Bewildered" is full of those who quit before the race was over, or who resigned from life before they finished the game.

One day a father was talking to a friend about his son, who had caused him great heartache. The friend said, "If he were my son, I would kick him out!" The father thought for a moment, then said, "Yes, if he were your son, so would I. But he is not your son, he is *mine* and I can't do it!"

The person you choose to be your shock absorber must have compassion and a heart of love and understanding for *your* need. Finding a solid Christian friend to talk to is top priority; seek out one who has an exemplary Christian life. Not that she is perfect, but you want to be sure that she isn't worse off than you are. How can she help you if she is all "hung up" herself?

Back-fence counseling today takes the form of a telephone because so often miles separate those who are the closest to us. If you can reach for the phone and call a friend who has most of the qualifications to serve as a solid confidante, this may be the provision for the emotional support you need to carry you through your emotional crisis. Believe me, speech is the magic key that will unlock excessive pressure and relieve pent-up emotions for parents. Talking to God in prayer is strengthening your faith, we know that. Talking to a friend strengthens your emotional tone.

So talk to God and keep your vertical relationship in good order. Then seek out a Christian friend to keep your horizontal relationship functioning. A specific order is involved in the restoration of a person to emotional and spiritual health, but that restoration process is to be carried out in a spirit of gentleness. This spirit also involves humility. An attitude of supportive kindness that says, "You know, I've got problems, too, and I want you to pray with me. Together we both are going to grow in Christ."

That verse in Galatians 6 which talks about "bearing one another's burdens" says to me that when the load gets too heavy to carry and one is being crushed by the load, it is time for a friend to jump in and say, "Hey, I'm here. I love you. I want to carry this load with you. I can't carry it for you, but I'll carry it *with* you, believing God for victory."

FOOTPRINTS

One night a man had a dream. He dreamed he was walking along the beach with the Lord. Across the sky flashed scenes from his life. For each scene he noticed two sets of footprints in the sand—one belonging to him, and the other to the Lord. When the last scene had flashed before him, he looked back at the footprints and noticed that many times along the path there was only one set of footprints in the sand. He also noticed that this happened during the lowest and saddest times in his life. This really bothered him and he questioned the Lord, "Lord, You said that once I decided to follow You, You would walk all the way, but I noticed that during the most troublesome times of my life, there was only one set of footprints. I don't understand why, when I needed You most, You deserted me." The Lord replied, "My precious, precious child, I love you and would never leave you. During your times of trial and suffering when you see only one set of footprints, *it was then that I carried you.*"

Author Unknown

Again, don't let foolish pride keep you from confiding in a Christian friend who can help you carry your emotional burden. Talking about your heartache with your friend, sifting your thoughts and feelings, chewing over your questions, your feelings and your conflicts again and again will help ventilate them. In this ventilation process, you will find that much of the pent-up poisonous feelings will dissolve.

Once you can get some emotional *balance* in your thinking, then you can begin making some practical plans for coping with your own reactions and reactions in the family. You will find the load is heavy when you are working it out on your own, but in sharing it with someone, the burden is made lighter.

Abraham Lincoln said, "I have been driven many times to my knees by the overwhelming conviction that I had nowhere else to go." Getting down on our knees is a method of getting us back on our feet. But when you need someone in the flesh with a warm hand to lay on your shoulder, you will appreciate the fact that a Christian friend possesses "a mind through which Christ thinks, a heart through which Christ loves, a voice through which Christ speaks, and a hand through which Christ helps."

Moving from the panic button to the holding pattern, you will need all these avenues of strength. So ignore your phone bill, which may look like the national debt. If your friend can help to share your panic and empathize with you through this crisis, consider it to be God's way of letting His love flow through to you.

God's love is that adhesive glue which will put the pieces of your shattered life back together again. It can come through a friend who understands, a letter of encouragement or praise, or in a taped message you might hear. All can be anointed with God's love. It is there, available for you. God's love is all around. Love cannot be forced, cannot be coaxed or teased. It comes down from heaven—unasked and unsought; may it not be unreceived.

13

What to Do When There Is Nothing You Can Do!

There will be a day after you first learn your child is a homosexual when you will feel that God who was once with you "left and went home early." You will feel so alone, and you will have to battle some crushing emotional feelings of isolation. Here are some practical ways to "peel yourself off the ceiling" when you are frozen on the panic button and vibrating from wall to wall.

1. Remember that *yours is not a solitary case,* but only one in a giant minority scattered across the world. If parents could recall instances when friends had heard similar disclosures made by their children, the jolt would be far less. Homosexuality does not negate parental love any more than God negates His love for His children when they fall into sin. He still loves them. After kids tell their parents of their homosexual involvement, at least their own inner struggle has been externalized. Let me add, very *few* kids actually *tell* their parents of their homosexuality. Parents find out, as I did, in other ways, and this sometimes com-

132

pounds the situation because the information was "flushed out" of the child, rather than shared when he (or she) was ready.

2. *Your child is still your child.* Knowing he is involved in homosexuality does not erase all the joy and blessing he has been to you over the years when he was growing up. His sexuality is only a part of his life. Does your knowledge of his problem mean that you cannot be the same loving mother you were a few hours *before* you knew this? Has he changed? Isn't this the same child you would do *anything* for?—even to giving your life to save his? Where is the love and compassion which you displayed so easily before? Character is not made in a crisis—it is exhibited in one.

If your child reveals a piece of his own life to you, this is an expression of deep trust. Making this disclosure to you is probably one of the major decisions of his life. Your reaction will be long remembered. What a terrific opportunity for parents to show their loyalty and allegiance to their child when they are first aware he is caught in this awful dilemma. Should the knowledge of it somehow cripple our ability to show our allegiance to him?

Get across to him that you love him *no matter what.* This unconditional love is what you must communicate to him. Though you hate his sin because God does and because it will hurt him, regardless of his condition you love him.

Right here I want to insert an account of an incident which illustrates the need for real unconditional love. The phone rang in a wealthy Boston home. On the other end of the line was a son who had just returned from Vietnam and was calling from California. The boy said to his mother, "I just called to tell you that I wanted to bring a buddy home with me."

His mother said, "Sure, bring him along for a few days."

"But Mother, there is something you need to know about this boy. One leg is gone, one arm is missing, one eye's gone and his face is quite disfigured. Is it all right if I bring him home?"

His mother said, "Bring him home for just a few days."

The son said, "You didn't understand me, Mother. I want to bring him home to live with us." As the mother began to make excuses about embarrassment and what people would think—the phone clicked.

A few hours later that mother answered the phone again. The police sergeant at the other end said, "We have found the body of a boy with one arm, one leg, one eye, and a mangled face; he just killed himself with a shot in the head. The identification papers on the body say he is your son."

When men live without unconditional love, we see one bad scene after another. Keep your love flowing to your child in every possible way you can demonstrate it. It will assure him and insure you. Your unconditional love will serve as a reminder to him of God's love for him. And keeping the love flowing will also prevent stagnation and bitterness from settling in your own heart.

Proverbs 27:22 says, "You can't separate a rebel from his foolishness though you crush him to powder" (TLB). You will feel like doing that if you have normal parental reactions to this emotionally charged situation. Ask God to drain off your anger and resentments and pull the plug on all the overwhelming negative feelings you are experiencing. Ask Him to replace them with a river of love that will flow to the child who is hurting as much as you are.

If he is caught in deep sin, unwilling to change, or even if he is too uptight to discuss it with you, make him aware that your love does not depend on his behavior. You can love him *because* of his struggle, not *in spite of* it.

3. *Keep in close fellowship with the Lord.* Sometimes situations like this *drive* people to God. You want to be an overcomer; this is an opportunity for you

to overcome. If you were not in fellowship with the Lord before this happened, you can be now. Praise the Lord in the *midst* of the situation, knowing God is able to restore your child to complete fellowship. Be ready to welcome your child with open arms, no questions asked. Remember when the prodigal came home, his father didn't ask, "Well, what is your explanation for where you have been?" He didn't expect the son to account for his foolish living. Instead, he just opened his arms to him and welcomed him home, this dirty, undone, smelling-of-hogs son. Can you do that to your child? You had better learn how if you want a restoration!

4. Make your continual reflection be *"Praise the Lord anyhow!"* This situation will be used by God to purify your life and make your family united in serving the Lord. Trials strengthen the bonds, making them as strong as cables. Let this trial deepen your faith and make you precious metal for the Master's use, having the dross removed by the fire.

Above, all, wrap the child in love and present him to the Lord for restoration. This commitment to the Lord will free you to pray for the healing power of the Holy Spirit to invade and liberate him. Keep Romans 8:28 forever in your heart. God's promise that "all things work together for good" even when things seem to be shattered should take a high position on the priority list of verses on suffering. Saturate yourself with God's Word so that when you awaken in the middle of the night with anxiety symptoms, you will hear the voice of God whisper to you, "My child, this will all work out for good because you love Me and are called to my purpose." This saturation with helpful verses will be the kind of inner urging from the Lord that will promote healing for you.

Think about this: "In love's service, only the wounded can serve, for they alone understand the cry of the bleeding heart." This shattered feeling will one day be gone, and in its place will be a heart of love that will minister to others whom God will bring into your life because you have overcome this cup of suffering and survived!

5. *Study these verses on anxiety and worry:* Psalm 16:11; 37:1, 7: 43:5; Isaiah 41:10; Proverbs 16:7; Matthew 6:31–34; Philippians 4:6–9, 19; 2 Thessalonians 3:3; 1 Peter 5:7.

14

God's Special Adhesive Glue and How to Use It!

As I have mentioned in previous chapters, there are only *two* things you can do for your child who has chosen the homosexual lifestyle: love him unconditionally and pray for him. When you are assured that is the extent of the help you can be to him, then you can concentrate on practical ways to keep your family glued together during this crisis.

First of all, there is no simple or slick advice and there are no easy steps to take out of the blackness which often envelops parents after they learn their child has labeled himself "homosexual." However, some of the following suggestions may help accelerate your healing process as a family. They may enable you to pass through the initial shock stage and then move into the coping stage, when your shock has been replaced by compassion. Parents must learn to "unkink their hoses" so that compassion can flow to the child who is desperately in need of it, now more than ever. Here are some ways to express that love, in the process finding emotional healing yourself.

1. Keep the communication channel *open*. Reassure your child verbally of your love and care for him. God is in charge and has not negated him because of his sin. Think of your child as a lost sheep—hurting, caught in the brambles, and needing love and direction. Your love and concern will be a lifeline to him right now while he is struggling with his identity crisis.

2. Stop blaming yourself! You cannot accept the blame for the choice your child has made. You probably did the best job you could in raising him. You must realize that studies show the causes of homosexuality to be so diversified that no *one* factor can fully be identified as the root cause. Stop playing the "blame game." Instead, savor the good news that *Jesus was nailed to a cross so that* you *could stop nailing yourself to a cross!*

3. This shock is very similar to a time of deep mourning, particularly if your child has removed himself from your home. One of Satan's subtle tricks is to disturb and cut off the peace and love of the *whole* family through the sin of one member. Give your child to God, wrap him in love through daily contacts with him, if possible. Then get down to the business of moving *out* of this panic period and into a productive situation for the rest of the family.

4. Don't try to give advice. Unless you have read extensively on the subject, you don't have a rounded picture of homosexuality anyway. Just communicate love to your child and then set out to become informed about how others have found the way out of homosexuality with God's help.

5. To accelerate your move through the shock stage, get yourself a shoe box and begin collecting verses, poems, inspirational thoughts, anything which lightens this entire unreal situation for you. Unless you can get some balance in your life, you will remain frozen in the initial shock stage. This "Joy Box" will be your inspiration. You will find that soon

you are gathering enough strength to carry yourself through the days when the depression has settled on you like a thick fog.

6. If you experience the anxiety symptoms of chest pain and nausea, they will probably remain with you the first few months after you learn your child is a homosexual. The biggest shock wave will be the plaque of unreal emotions. Accepting them means you recognize anxiety symptoms for what they are. Remind yourself that "this too shall pass."

7. Get yourself a *big* spatula. Keep it in a prominent place to remind yourself that you are going to be "peeling *yourself* off the ceiling" a lot in the coming months. There really is no other warm, human hand to assist you—only your own hanging onto that spatula. You are not needed up there, splattered on the ceiling with self-pity and blame. Your family needs you with your feet solidly planted on the floor and your mind and body functioning normally. You have no time for mental blocks right now. Remember, the definition of a mental block is "the street where several psychiatrists live" and you have the Greatest Psychiatrist of all on *your* street right now.

8. Make your home a warm, loving place. It should be a safe place for everyone in the family, much more than a "filling station." Make it a place where each member feels accepted, loved and free from condemnation. Home should be where you can be silent and still be heard, where you can ask and find out who you are, where people laugh with you about yourself, where sorrow is divided and joy is multiplied, where we share and love and grow, where we can come and have our batteries recharged when our spirits are run down.

9. Develop a sense of humor. If one is not innate in you, then borrow, or create one! It is imperative! A sense of humor is the pole that adds balance to your steps as you walk the tight-rope of life. You will have feelings of a pendulum swinging from honor to hope,

and the complete devastation engulfing you at times will choke out your humor. But keep working at it. All crisis situations can be endured more easily when you are able to inject some lightheartedness into each day. (Besides, keeping sunshine in your heart will help keep wrinkles from your face—you want to be well preserved as you grow older, not pickled!)

10. Praise the Lord in the *midst* of your situation. You cannot thank Him *for* it specifically, but praise Him for what you know He will bring *out* of it. If you can praise Him in the middle of your trial, then your home and your mind will remain intact. Make this a time of growing and refining. With some insight and real honesty in learning how others cope with this, you can keep your home from being blown like a straw house in the wind. We know that God can, and will, and is doing a work in lives, transforming them and changing them. We cannot give the final score on a life until the game is over—and it isn't even half-time yet. Remember, "Be patient. God isn't finished with your child yet." You can decide to go through this trial or to *grow* through it. Start now to believe that this has come through God's special filter of love and that He knows the end results it will produce in your life. He makes beauty from ashes in lives, constantly.

11. If your child has left home, keep the flow of loving-kindness going to him wherever he is. I've heard that "kindness is giving someone a piece of bread and butter, but loving-kindness is putting peanut butter and jelly on it." Give love in abundance and do it *in style*.

12. Be thankful for other young people God will send into your life who will allow you to demonstrate love to them. Keep love flowing from you no matter what! This will help to keep bitterness and harshness out of your heart so that when your child returns home, you can envelop him with a healing flow of love to restore the relationship.

13. God places a great value on suffering. The

Scriptures tell us that suffering is a necessary ingredient in our spiritual development (1 Pet. 2:21). God says we are to glory in—not endure—suffering and tribulation. Concentrating on that will help you keep your sanity. The following statement about suffering will be meaningful to you after you have progressed through the coping stage and are on the road to survival. This truth will help you absorb it—over and over—like a record:

> There is no oil without squeezing the olives.
> No wine without pressing the grapes.
> No fragrance without crushing the flowers, and
> No real JOY without sorrow.

15

Peeling Them Off the Ceiling—With a Spatula of Love

Some weeks passed and the calm mantle of assurance that God was working in Larry's life had been fully translated into my thinking. After all, there are only two things we can do for our kids when they grow up: we can pray for them, and we can love them; the *rest* is in God's hands.

Our contacts with Larry were becoming easier and more frequent, and I was so grateful that I had survived a situation that had left others with tremendous residual depression. I had a deep desire to love other parents who were going through the experience and trauma from which I'd just emerged.

In fact, I felt such love and an overflowing river of care for others which I had not possessed before. The Melodyland Hotline Center rejoiced with me that we had experienced a partial restoration with Larry, and I had frequent contacts with the Hotline regarding some ideas I had for starting a caring group for the parents of homosexuals. However, all the parents I knew of were not in the immediate area or were so distraught they were not ready for any type of group situation.

One day I got a call at home from a counselor at the Hotline. He said there was an urgent call from a mother who lived near me who had just learned her son was homosexual. She was drinking heavily, taking pills and threatening to drive herself and her son over a cliff on Highway 39. This hardly sounded like something for a beginner like me to "peel off the ceiling"! Just hearing of all the anguish she was going through from the counselor brought back some of my early struggles of a year ago with sanity and insanity. I had learned to swim now. I could pull someone else out of the drowning situation or, I could just go on and make new friends and contacts and wave the year 1975 into the past, since I had returned to the land of beginning again. No, of course not! God was bringing good out of this terrible last year.

And this woman was really in need of some bandages—cables would be more appropriate. Margaret was apprehensive and afraid to come to see me. She was so nervous when she finally did come over. She walked around the room in circles, too wrought up to sit down. Her speech was incoherent, her eyes were wild and swollen; she was too upset to work and unable to function in her role as wife and mother. She was about as "far out" of reality as one could get, and I knew that only God could bring her out of this state of emotional panic.

She frantically paced the floor and suffered nausea (as I had a year ago). Finally she calmed down enough to admit she knew nothing about homosexuality. She had come from a Catholic background and was sheltered and protected from the reality of life in many ways.

The story of how God worked in Margaret's family is exciting! Her entire family are now Christians, all serving the Lord, and her son who had the homosexual problem got involved with our group and made some

good solid Christian friends who are "caring." He has
made his decision to come out of that life and let God
control his life now. God has transformed that empty
godless home with no goals to a beautiful lighthouse
where other young people can come and share together. The love which God placed in her heart for
these young people is like the river which God placed
in mine.

Margaret was my first test. I was able to help this
fractured, shattered, completely out-of-whack
woman, so close to suicide and emotionally like melted
wax, find her way out of a living hell. What a miracle
took place as I saw her use God's tools for healing. She
started learning scriptures and listening to tapes
which helped her to grow and began attending a good,
solid Bible class where she learned the Word.

Since she lived only a couple miles from me, Margaret came over some evenings just to have fellowship
and share with me. Sometimes she would come in her
housecoat and just sit on the floor and listen as I coun-
seled other mothers on the telephone. (By this time I
was helping others.) She would see the picture of how
this ministry is like throwing a stone in the water—
the ripples go out and out and we don't know how
many lives are touched.

Months passed, and Margaret grew strong and
able in the Lord. God's adhesive bound up her shattered life, and she began to feel along with me that we
needed to have a group of mothers come together and
minister to one another in love.

The name SPATULA, which evolved for this ministry for parents, is quite unique. One evening I was
in a meeting with several leaders at Hotline Counseling Center, each of whom were being asked what they
needed to help their ministry function more ade-
quately. When my turn came, I responded, "Well, I
need about a dozen big spatulas to pull these frantic
mothers down off the ceiling when they first learn
their kid is a homosexual!" Everyone laughed, and

that was the beginning of the name. We started with only a few mothers. As the group grew in numbers and maturity, I felt the Lord propelling us with real love.

SPATULA is not an encounter group. It is not a Bible study, nor a probing, problem-solving, pat-answer group. It is a loving, caring group of parents who are hurting, who find that they can come and share their feelings with each other—their down times and their triumphs, their heartaches and their wounds which are still very fresh and painful.

After our group started, a few young people who were struggling to break out of the gay lifestyle began coming to the meetings. The first one was a former lesbian who had married and had a son. She called in desperation, thinking that now her son might be a homosexual. It was a frantic, panic-stricken woman who came to our meeting that night. She had experienced the gay life, then married and been divorced, and she couldn't cope with the thought that her son might be a homosexual. She declared to the group that she would rather put him in the oven than see him in the homosexual lifestyle.

Since the meetings were primarily for mothers of homosexuals, I didn't know how parents would react to the inclusion of ex-homosexuals in the group, but so much love abounds in that group that you feel it when you come into the room. We don't have to instruct people to be caring or concerned. They just are!

SPATULA is a whole story in itself—with its victories, its triumphs, its joys. It encompasses the dreams and reality of so many hurting people. SPATULA reflects the wisdom of Ecclesiastes 4:9–10, as we have surely found that "two can accomplish more than twice as much as one, for the results can be much better. If one falls, the other pulls him up; but if a man falls when he is alone, he is in trouble" (TLB).

The key verse which we give each person who comes into the group is Philippians 4:8: "Finally, brethren, whatever is true, whatever is honorable, whatever is just, whatever is pure, whatever is lovely, whatever is gracious, if there is any excellence, if there is anything worthy of praise, think about these things" (RSV).

Yes, SPATULA—to bring parents down from the ceiling and the wall—is a winner! It works! It has blossomed and produced fruit. God has propelled this ministry into an outreach which is touching a hurting world. SPATULA is mending lives—scraping parents off the wall and then healing their wounds. The verse which defines the purpose of the group is Isaiah 61:1: "to bind up the brokenhearted."

Spatula Ministries
P.O. Box 444
La Habra, CA 90631

16

Insanity Is Hereditary—We Get It from Our Kids

When we brought Barney home from the hospital twenty years ago, on Christmas morning, he was bundled in a bright red, fluffy Christmas stocking which the hospital provided for all babies going home on Christmas Day.

What a joyous time to bring home a beautiful baby boy! The first few months were hectic, because he had colic, which I knew nothing about (except that if my first child had had it, there wouldn't have been any others to follow!). By the time he was a year old, we actually had to *pay a* neighbor child to come over to the house and jounce Barney so we could eat our dinner in peace. I jounced him for so long that even after he outgrew colic, I would catch myself jouncing the basket of groceries when in a supermarket.

"Trouble" seemed to be his middle name when he was smaller, and when he painted the neighbor's front porch black one day, I had more than an inkling that raising Barney was going to be no small chore.

With me in the supermarket one day when the

147

turnstiles were jammed with customers, he was playing with a dime, and inadvertently it rolled down between the connections on the revolving check-out line. Suddenly everything stopped. The checkers couldn't check, the lights went out, and the store was in complete darkness. His dime had gotten into the mechanism and shorted out the entire electrical system. So from the beginning I got the impression that life with Barney was going to be exciting. I really had to keep on my toes with him to keep from getting out-shuffled.

When he was about ten, and I was working, I would leave a list of chores for each boy to do after school. I tried to divide the tasks evenly, but one day Larry complained that he had so much to do on his list he could not possibly complete it all. We compared notes and found that Barney had made a typewritten list of *all* the chores for the *others* to do; then he signed the notes "MOM," put lipstick on himself and blotted it on the notes just as I always did. How laboriously he must have worked on typing those notes and applying the lipstick before any one of us caught on to his little scheme!

Barney was such a charmer that he got all through school using just one book for his book reports, *The Cross and the Switchblade*. We said he developed a cauliflower ear—not from boxing, but from continual use of the phone in his teens.

Some years ago when wigs first came into vogue, I had bought one and placed it on the styrofoam head on the dresser, waiting for an opportunity to wear it. Barney answered the phone one day when someone called for me, and his answer was, "She's not home, but she hasn't gone far, because her head is here!"

He is the one who would volunteer me to be room mother, or den mother, to "cook" 3,000 marbles in the oven and then "crack" them in cold water to make trivets for 5th grade Christmas presents.

Tim was particularly close to Barney, and after his death we noticed a real change in Barney's personality. He lost his interest in church and old friends and began to make friends with kids whom we knew were into marijuana and drugs. I overlooked some of his unresponsiveness to us because I knew he was grieving for Tim, but I was concerned that his friends were obviously not those we would have chosen for him.

During his high school years we had the scare many parents have when the phone rings and a police officer calls saying, "Your son was at the swap and marijuana was found in the car." When the call came Bill and I frantically dressed and drove up to the swap to bring him home and find out which of his friends he could blame. He never really had any big problem with what his friends were into, but that was a miracle because at that point he had no incentive to improve himself. He was quiet in his high school years and spent most of his time working around the garage with his friends, replacing parts on dirt bikes and motors.

During the eleven months when Larry was gone, the house suddenly was very large with only three of us moving around. I was such a zombie during that time, it was really more like two and one half persons moving around. Barney says he had known about Larry's homosexual problem before I found it out; and being the type of personality he is, very non-judgmental, Barney said nothing. His attitude was "live and let live." Looking back, perhaps he took the most sensible approach to the whole thing.

It was during those months that Barney cared for me in such a gentle way. For no special reason he would come in and give me a hug and tell me he was glad he had me for his mother. It almost made me wonder if he had gotten another ticket and was buttering me up before he broke the big news again. (All his traffic violations were minor and he never got any fines for them, only reprimands from the traffic court.) Other times there would be thoughtful notes left around on the first of each month, with a familiar scrawl saying, "You are the best mom in the world." All this showed that he was feeling and caring though he would not reveal his true self on a one-to-one basis. He loved the outdoors, windmills, feeling the breeze in his face while riding on a dirt bike, and standing in front of the refrigerator with both doors open waiting for something to jump out at him.

Barney suffered through much of the family trauma in a silent, quieter way than the others did. He kept himself busy with making wire gifts in school and using his skills to create decorative things for me and other friends. His quiet ways, which make him so easy to live with, and his consistency of mood, which permits him to "wear well," make Barney a real strength in a time of need. He helped me during those eleven months, encouraged me, and has shown his love in many tangible ways.

All during his years at Christian schools he cared little for actual studying or learning. However, he always got straight A's in Bible—not because he studied much but because learning verses was part of the training, and I would go over his memory work with him fiercely each week. Fiercely is the only word applicable because I was fierce if he didn't learn them properly. As I was getting ready for work, he would come in and flop down on the bed and begin learning his verses for the week. I knew he was out playing ball after school and never doing any homework, but at that time in the morning when I was getting myself together for work, he was hiding God's Word in his heart. I grew up with a lot of Scripture in me because it was drilled into me that we had to hide it away to have a big reserve in times of trouble. Knowing the Scripture probably was the greatest strength which carried me through the traumas. I had a lot of deposits in my spiritual bank, and the resources from the memory work my parents had built into me as a child were great.

So, because of our time together in the morning,

Barney knew his memory verses; he knew the plan of salvation, and received the Lord when he was a child. However, during his teen years I saw no evidence of a transformed life and kept praying that God would send along a Christian girl whom he could love, and who would influence him toward a total commitment to Christ. Three years ago, God sent a beautiful dark-haired little Christian girl into his life. She took Barney to Maranatha concerts at Calvary Chapel where he went forward and dedicated his life to the Lord. (We had dedicated him as a baby, but this was his own decision.) This lovely Shannon, who was straight from the Lord to us, has brought out qualities in Barney which were hidden deep inside. Now Shannon and Barney together have established a home centered on God's principles.

The high point in my life in relation to Barney happened just a few months ago: Larry was graduating from college with honors and all of us were going to the graduation. However, Barney had just had his wisdom teeth out and was really suffering the after-effects. Instead of going, he wrote Larry a note on the back of his graduation card. I was so thrilled with what he said to Larry that I asked Barney if I could share it in this book. I think it is perhaps the most unusual tribute I have ever received:

> To Bro, who I want very much to prosper for all you've gone through. It should be a great future ahead. The one you owe it to is Mom, so do I. She is *one hell of a mom* and I'm sure you know no one could beat her. She loves you and me so much it hurts her, but she is happy for both of us. Mom needs your love, Larry. She loves you very much. I'm sure what happened is in the past, and I love you cause you are my bro, but Mom needs your love as a son. Sorry about my writing, but I am all buzzed cause I got my wisdom teeth pulled and don't feel too good. Keep in touch. I am proud of

you more than anything. Never look back, but always ahead. I'm with ya.

Love,
Barney.

In all his twenty years of living, I don't think I ever received such a high compliment from Barney. "One hell of a mom" might not be your usual evangelical phraseology, but I would be honored and delighted that my son Barney thought that of me.

Barney has added so much enjoyment to our lives. We never know what comment to expect from him. He has an old 1957 Ford, and recently when Bill celebrated his fifty-seventh birthday, though Barney never was real quick in math, he came up with how neat it was that Bill was the same age as his car!

That baby in the bright red Christmas stocking grew up to be a fine, loving man, who thinks he has "one hell of a mom"—which is O.K. with me.

17

Where Does a Mother Go to Resign?

There is no magic place to go when we face insur-
mountable problems. There is no never-never land,
there is no place where "troubles melt like lemon
drops, way above the chimney tops." We may have to
live with mountains that will not move, but we can
face the inevitable and realize that we have greater
reserves and resources than we thought possible.

We can never get our lives together until we stop
looking back; we must "launch out into the deep" with
God's promises. Hurting makes us want to look back.
When tragedy is irreversible, then you must begin
working your way through whatever must be faced.
Don't hesitate to open every floodgate, cross every
bridge that comes. Accept the sovereign hand of God
to sort out the possibilities. Remember that regardless
of the turning of the tides, God alone is the source of
your adequacy.

Resign? Me? Never! *Resign from a wonderful husband who has supported me through all this trauma?
Resign from Larry whom God has his hand on and
who, in time, will return to the Lord? Resign from Barney and his darling wife, Shannon, who have just*

154

made me a grandmother to a beautiful little girl? Resign from this ministry which already has brought so much fulfillment and reward? Resign from seeing parents find reconciliation and restoration with their children through unconditional love?

I don't want to resign. I want to recruit others to share in this ministry, sharing God's love, letting it flow to hurting people, being one who can be called a "wound healer."

That was the "all-things-work-together-for-good" that God brought out of this suffering to share the insights which I received when I was there where others are now—hurting, bleeding, dying inside.

But I did survive! I was a winner—like the song says, "Hallelujah, we win, I read the back of the book and we win!" SPATULA is to help people be winners in this battle with Satan for our children. There is a whole world out there that is in need of what we have learned, of what I have shared with you in this book that illustrates God's faithfulness. He brought me through the deep water without letting me drown. He held me up when my mind and emotions were torn apart by tragedy. He gave me the gift of *joy* which made it possible to share with others the good things God was going to do for them also.

I'm off the ceiling and back into the flow of life where it is exciting and where miracles are happening in lives all around. Broken lives are being mended, families are being restored and God is at work. Who would want to miss out on a minute of the exciting ways God is moving today? Not me! I can live in the nasty now and now until He takes me to the sweet bye and bye—and happily, with joy bubbling up in my heart, flowing out from that river of love He put there to share in other restorations. Thank God there is no place to resign—no way, nowhere. Praise God for His faithfulness in taking us through the deep water and not letting us drown. And for letting us survive so we can, in turn, help others who are floundering.

Epilogue

In May of 1986 Barbara received a phone call from her son that he wanted to come over to bring her a "mothers' day present." She was delighted as it had been so many years of painful separation and estrangement since that sad day at Disneyland in 1975.

Her son Larry came to the house and with tears in his eyes asked for forgiveness for the eleven years of pain he had caused the family. He said he had rededicated his life to the Lord the previous week and had taken all the symbols of his "old life" to a fireplace and burned them . . . and when they were burning he felt a complete sense of release and CLEAN BEFORE THE LORD FOR THE FIRST TIME IN ELEVEN YEARS.

THIS WAS HIS MOTHERS' DAY PRESENT TO BARBARA.

Both Larry and Barbara learned many painful lessons during their eleven year struggle.

LARRY:

Life is an intricate pattern of relationships . . . sometimes God uses problems to bring out good qualities in us. Satan capitalizes on fear and ignorance— the very things God does not want in our lives. In times of family crisis we need to remember an all-important truth—GOD IS IN CONTROL.

If we put our complete trust in God we will fear nothing. We must trust in Him and learn of His ways—herein lies wisdom. As Christians we should be able to transcend tragedy—not reacting out of fear, anger, etc., but responding in unconditional love as we rest in the assurance of God's faithfulness.

BARBARA:

As parents we must remember we are not responsible for our children's choices. But we must examine ourselves in times of crisis and admit to our failures—then put them aside.

God does go after the prodigals. As parents, it is our job to love our children; it is God's job to bring to pass His work of salvation in their lives.

It was a long, painful eleven years of WAITING for this miracle to happen, but now there is a true restoration in the family. The broken pieces have been mended; the hearts that were torn and bleeding with raw edges have been healed; the "hope deferred" has come to pass and there is life and joy in God's promises.